THE TALE OF TAMIL KINGS AND QUEENS

J CHIDAMBARAM

This edition has been published in india by arrangement with Carson Books, UK

ISBN 9789355277565   MJP Publishers

All rights reserved   No. 44, Nallathambi Street,
Printed and bound in India   Triplicane, Chennai 600 005

MJP 1666   © Publishers, 2024

Publisher :   C. Janarthanan

CONTENTS

CHAPTER ONE

THE KINGDOM OF TAMILS

In the vibrant land of Tamil Nadu, rich in culture and history, there arose a line of extraordinary rulers whose tales have been etched in the annals of time. These stories, passed down through generations, speak of kings and queens who were not only powerful and wise but also compassionate and just. They ruled over their people with a blend of strength and kindness, leaving behind a legacy that continues to inspire even today.

In this book, "The Tale of Tamil Kings and Queens," we delve into the lives of these remarkable figures. Our journey begins with the Chola dynasty, a time when the land was united under the rule of mighty kings like Rajaraja Chola and Rajendra Chola. Their reigns marked a golden era of prosperity, military prowess, and cultural renaissance. Through their vision and leadership, the Chola Empire expanded its territories, established grand temples, and promoted trade and learning.

We will also explore the courageous life of Queen Velu Nachiyar, who valiantly fought against British colonial forces to reclaim her kingdom. Her story is one of resilience, intelligence, and unwavering determination. Alongside her, we meet King Karikala Chola, whose innovative spirit led to the construction of the Kallanai Dam, a marvel of ancient engineering that transformed the agricultural landscape of his kingdom.

Next, we turn our attention to Queen Mangammal, a ruler known for her wisdom and diplomatic acumen. In a time when the Mughal Empire's influence was spreading across India, Queen Mangammal managed to maintain the sovereignty and prosperity of Madurai through strategic alliances and shrewd negotiations. Her reign was marked by significant improvements in infrastructure, including roads, temples, and irrigation systems that benefited her people and fostered economic growth.

Education and culture flourished under these rulers. The Tamil kings and queens were not only warriors but also patrons of the arts and sciences. They understood that a strong, prosperous society required educated citizens and a rich cultural life. Schools and universities were established, attracting scholars from far and wide. The construction of grand temples like the Brihadeeswarar Temple in Thanjavur, initiated by Rajaraja Chola, stands as a testament to the architectural brilliance and cultural patronage of the Chola dynasty.

Justice and compassion were cornerstones of their leadership. Stories abound of these rulers disguising themselves to mingle with their subjects, understanding their grievances, and delivering fair judgments. King Rajendra Chola, for instance, was known for his open court sessions where anyone could present their case, ensuring that justice was accessible to all.

The military achievements of these rulers were not just about conquests. They forged strategic alliances and negotiated treaties to maintain peace and stability. Rajendra Chola's naval expeditions extended the empire's influence far beyond the Indian subcontinent, establishing Tamil dominance over the seas and fostering international trade relations.

Infrastructure and innovation were key to the prosperity of the Tamil kingdoms. King Karikala Chola's Kallanai Dam, built across the Kaveri River, is a prime example of such innovation. This ancient dam not only controlled floods but also ensured a stable water supply for agriculture, boosting the kingdom's food production and economic stability. The Chola kings also constructed extensive networks of roads, connecting distant parts of the empire and facilitating trade and communication.

Economic prosperity was a hallmark of these reigns. The Tamil rulers established bustling trade routes with distant lands, including Southeast Asia, China, and the Middle East. The ports of the Chola Empire were hubs of activity, welcoming merchants from across the world and enriching the kingdom through trade. These economic policies not only brought wealth but also cultural exchanges that enriched Tamil society.

The social and religious contributions of these rulers were profound. They were deeply involved in the construction and restoration of temples, which were not just places of worship but also centers of community life and learning. The grand festivals and rituals organized in these temples fostered a sense of unity and cultural pride among the people. Queen Velu Nachiyar's efforts to build alliances and support her people during her resistance against the British are a testament to the social commitment tof Tamil rulers.

Environmental stewardship was another significant aspect of their governance. Kings like Rajendra Chola implemented policies to protect natural resources, ensuring sustainable development. Forests were preserved, and wildlife was protected, reflecting a deep understanding of the importance of environmental conservation for the well-being of the kingdom.

The legacy of these Tamil kings and queens continues to resonate in modern times. Their principles of justice, compassion, innovation, and cultural patronage are timeless, offering valuable lessons for contemporary leaders and societies. The grand temples, inscriptions, and artifacts they left behind stand as enduring symbols of their reign and achievements.

In particular, the contributions of Rajaraja Chola and his son Rajendra Chola laid the foundation for a prosperous and culturally rich Tamil Nadu. The Brihadeeswarar Temple, a UNESCO World Heritage Site, remains a marvel of Chola architecture, attracting visitors and scholars from around the world. Rajendra Chola's conquests and administrative reforms expanded the empire's reach and influence, making it one of the most powerful and well-governed realms of its time.

Queen Velu Nachiyar's story is a powerful example of resistance and resilience. Her strategic acumen and leadership in the face of British colonial aggression continue to inspire those who fight for freedom and justice. The fortresses and monuments associated with her reign are revered as symbols of her indomitable spirit and dedication to her people.

Queen Mangammal's legacy in Madurai is marked by the infrastructure and administrative reforms she introduced. Her strategic alliances and diplomatic skills ensured the stability and prosperity of her kingdom during a turbulent period in history. The roads, temples, and public works she commissioned continue to benefit the people of Madurai, reflecting her far-sighted vision and commitment to public welfare.

For young readers, the stories of these Tamil kings and queens offer numerous valuable lessons. They teach us the importance of courage, wisdom, and compassion in leadership. Rajaraja Chola's dedication to learning and justice reminds us that true leadership requires both strength and intellect. Rajendra Chola's open court sessions emphasize the importance of fairness and accessibility in governance. Queen Velu Nachiyar's resilience in the face of adversity shows that determination and strategic thinking can overcome even the most formidable challenges.

These stories also highlight the significance of dreams and determination. From a young prince with aspirations of greatness to a legendary king who built an empire, Rajaraja Chola's journey teaches us that with hard work and perseverance, we can achieve our goals. Queen Velu Nachiyar's fight against colonial forces demonstrates the power of standing up for what is right, even when faced with overwhelming odds.

The tale of these Tamil rulers is not just a recounting of historical events but a celebration of values and principles that resonate across time. They encourage us to be just, kind, and wise in our actions and to strive for excellence in everything we do. By following their example, we can all contribute to building a better and more prosperous world.

As we conclude this introduction, let us embark on this journey through the pages of history, learning from the lives of the Tamil kings and queens who have shaped the rich cultural heritage of Tamil Nadu. Their stories will inspire us, teach us, and remind us of the enduring power of vision, leadership, and justice.

As we delve deeper into the tales of these illustrious Tamil rulers, it's essential to recognize the critical role of education and culture in their reigns. Education was seen as the foundation of a prosperous and enlightened society. The kings and queens of Tamil Nadu established numerous schools and learning centers, attracting scholars from far and wide. These institutions not only imparted knowledge but also fostered a spirit of inquiry and intellectual curiosity.

King Rajaraja Chola, for instance, was known for his patronage of education and the arts. He established the famous Vedic college in Thanjavur, where scholars studied ancient texts, astronomy, mathematics, and philosophy. This emphasis on learning created a vibrant intellectual community that contributed to the cultural richness of the Chola Empire. Similarly, Queen Mangammal supported the establishment of schools and libraries, ensuring that her subjects had access to education and knowledge.

Cultural patronage was another hallmark of Tamil kings and queens. They understood that a thriving cultural life was essential for a cohesive and prosperous society. The grand temples they built were not just places of worship but also centers of cultural activities. Festivals, music, dance, and drama performances were encouraged, reflecting the artistic talents and creativity of the people.

One of the most significant cultural contributions of the Chola dynasty was the development of the Tamil script and literature. The kings and queens supported poets, writers, and artists, leading to a flourishing of Tamil literature and art. The works of Tamil poets and scholars from this period continue to be celebrated for their literary excellence and artistic beauty.

The importance of justice and compassion in leadership cannot be overstated. The Tamil kings and queens were renowned for their fair and just rule, which earned them the respect and loyalty of their subjects. They believed that a ruler's duty was to serve the people and ensure their well-being. This principle guided their actions and decisions, creating a just and harmonious society.

King Rajendra Chola's open court sessions are a prime example of this commitment to justice. By allowing anyone to present their grievances, Rajendra ensured that justice was accessible to all, regardless of their status or background. This practice not only resolved conflicts but also reinforced the people's faith in their ruler's fairness and wisdom. Rajendra's judgments were known for their fairness and ingenuity, further solidifying his reputation as a just and compassionate king.

Queen Mangammal also exemplified justice and compassion in her rule. Her court was known for its transparency and fairness, and she personally oversaw many important cases. Her dedication to justice earned her the title of "The Wise Queen," reflecting her commitment to ensuring that her subjects were treated with fairness and dignity.

Military achievements and diplomacy were also critical aspects of their reigns. The Tamil rulers were skilled warriors and strategic diplomats, able to protect and expand their kingdoms while maintaining peace and stability. King Rajendra Chola's naval expeditions to Southeast Asia and the establishment of diplomatic relations with other kingdoms showcased his strategic brilliance and diplomatic acumen. These efforts not only expanded the empire's influence but also brought wealth and prosperity through trade.

Infrastructure and innovation were integral to the success and prosperity of the Tamil kingdoms. The rulers understood that a well-developed infrastructure was essential for the economic and social development of their realm. They invested heavily in building roads, bridges, and irrigation systems, which facilitated trade, agriculture, and communication.

King Karikala Chola's construction of the Kallanai Dam is a testament to the innovative spirit of Tamil rulers. This ancient dam, built over 2,000 years ago, remains one of the oldest water regulation structures in the world. It was designed to divert the floodwaters of the Kaveri River, ensuring a stable water supply for irrigation. The Kallanai Dam transformed the agricultural landscape, boosting food production and ensuring the prosperity of the kingdom.

Economic prosperity and trade were other vital aspects of their reigns. The Tamil rulers established extensive trade networks, connecting their kingdoms with distant lands. The ports of the Chola Empire, such as Nagapattinam and Kaveripattinam, were bustling centers of trade, welcoming merchants from Southeast Asia, China, the Middle East, and beyond. These trade relations brought immense wealth to the kingdom, enriching its people and fostering cultural exchanges.

The social and religious contributions of the Tamil rulers were equally significant. They were deeply committed to the welfare of their subjects and worked tirelessly to improve their lives. They built temples, tanks, and rest houses, ensuring that the people had access to essential amenities. The temples, in particular, played a central role in the community, serving as places of worship, learning, and social gatherings.

Environmental stewardship was another critical aspect of their governance. The Tamil kings and queens recognized the importance of preserving natural resources and promoting sustainable development. They implemented policies to protect forests, conserve water, and maintain ecological balance. King Rajendra Chola, for example, introduced measures to protect the rivers and ensure their cleanliness, reflecting a deep understanding of environmental conservation.

The enduring legacy of these Tamil rulers continues to inspire and guide us in modern times. Their principles of justice, compassion, innovation, and cultural patronage remain relevant today, offering valuable lessons for contemporary leaders and societies. The grand temples, inscriptions, and artifacts they left behind stand as enduring symbols of their reign and achievements.

King Rajaraja Chola's establishment of the Brihadeeswarar Temple and his son Rajendra Chola's expansion of the empire laid the foundation for a prosperous and culturally rich Tamil Nadu. Queen Velu Nachiyar's resistance against British colonial forces and her efforts to build alliances and support her people during times of struggle are powerful examples of resilience and determination. Queen Mangammal's administrative reforms and infrastructure projects in Madurai continue to benefit the people, reflecting her visionary leadership.

For young readers, the stories of these Tamil kings and queens offer numerous valuable lessons. They teach us the importance of courage, wisdom, and compassion in leadership. They inspire us to dream big, work hard, and strive for excellence in everything we do. By following their example, we can all contribute to building a better and more prosperous world.

As we reflect on the lives and achievements of these remarkable rulers, it's essential to appreciate their holistic approach to governance. They understood that true leadership encompassed not only military strength and political acumen but also a deep commitment to the welfare of their people. Their reigns were characterized by a balance of power and compassion, ensuring that their kingdoms thrived both economically and socially.

The Tamil kings and queens placed a strong emphasis on community involvement and participation. They believed that the well-being of the kingdom depended on the active engagement of its citizens. This philosophy was evident in their policies, which encouraged local self-governance and empowered village councils to make decisions on matters affecting their communities. This approach not only ensured smooth administration but also fostered a sense of responsibility and pride among the people.

The impact of their leadership extended beyond their lifetimes. The values they upheld—justice, fairness, compassion, and innovation—were passed down through generations, influencing the governance and culture of Tamil Nadu for centuries. Their stories have been immortalized in literature, art, and folklore, serving as a source of inspiration for future leaders.

The Tamil rulers' contributions to art and culture were profound. They were patrons of music, dance, literature, and architecture, creating a rich cultural legacy that continues to be celebrated today. The temples they built, adorned with intricate sculptures and carvings, stand as monuments to their artistic vision and devotion. These cultural achievements not only enriched their own society but also influenced neighboring regions, spreading the legacy of Tamil art and culture far and wide.

The economic policies of the Tamil rulers were instrumental in ensuring the prosperity of their kingdoms. They promoted trade and commerce, established markets, and supported artisans and craftsmen. The ports of the Chola Empire were bustling centers of activity, attracting traders from across the world. These economic activities brought wealth and resources into the kingdom, which were then used to fund public works and social welfare projects.

One of the most remarkable aspects of their reigns was their commitment to social welfare. The Tamil kings and queens took a keen interest in the well-being of their subjects, implementing policies that improved living conditions and ensured access to essential services. They built hospitals, schools, and rest houses, providing for the needs of the people and fostering a sense of community and mutual support.

The emphasis on environmental stewardship by Tamil rulers was a testament to their foresight and understanding of sustainable development. They recognized that the prosperity of their kingdoms was closely linked to the health of the natural environment. By implementing policies to conserve forests, protect water sources, and maintain ecological balance, they ensured the long-term sustainability of their resources.

As we conclude this introduction, we are reminded of the timeless values and principles that guided the Tamil kings and queens. Their dedication to justice, compassion, innovation, and cultural patronage continues to inspire us today. Their stories serve as a beacon of hope and a reminder that true leadership is about serving others and striving for the greater good.

Let us embark on this journey through the pages of history, learning from the lives of these extraordinary rulers who have shaped the rich cultural heritage of Tamil Nadu. Their tales will inspire us, teach us, and remind us of the enduring power of vision, leadership, and justice.

As we explore the lives and achievements of these Tamil kings and queens, it is crucial to understand the profound impact of their contributions on the society and culture of their time. The grand temples they built were not only architectural marvels but also centers of social and cultural life. These temples played a vital role in the community, hosting festivals, ceremonies, and gatherings that brought people together and strengthened social bonds.

The Brihadeeswarar Temple, commissioned by Rajaraja Chola, is a prime example of this. It stands as a testament to the architectural and engineering prowess of the Chola dynasty. The temple's towering vimana (tower) and intricate sculptures are a reflection of the artistic excellence and cultural richness of the period. The temple also served as a center of learning, where scholars and artists could gather to exchange ideas and advance their knowledge.

Queen Velu Nachiyar's story is a powerful example of leadership and resilience. Her strategic acumen and unwavering determination in the face of British colonial aggression are a testament to her courage and intelligence. Her efforts to build alliances and support her people during times of struggle highlight her dedication to her kingdom and her people. Her legacy continues to inspire those who fight for justice and freedom.

Queen Mangammal's administrative and diplomatic achievements were instrumental in maintaining the stability and prosperity of Madurai. Her infrastructure projects, including the construction of roads and irrigation systems, facilitated trade and agriculture, boosting the economy and improving the quality of life for her subjects. Her strategic alliances and diplomatic skills ensured the kingdom's security during a turbulent period in history.

The Tamil kings and queens understood the importance of environmental conservation and sustainable development. Their policies to protect forests, conserve water, and maintain ecological balance were ahead of their time, reflecting a deep understanding of the interdependence between humans and nature. These efforts ensured the long-term sustainability of their resources, allowing their kingdoms to thrive for generations.

King Rajendra Chola's reign was marked by significant environmental initiatives. He implemented measures to protect the rivers and ensure their cleanliness, recognizing the importance of water conservation for agriculture and daily life. His policies to preserve forests and wildlife reflected a commitment to maintaining ecological balance and protecting natural resources.

The legacy of these Tamil rulers continues to inspire and guide us in modern times. Their principles of justice, compassion, innovation, and cultural patronage remain relevant today, offering valuable lessons for contemporary leaders and societies. The grand temples, inscriptions, and artifacts they left behind stand as enduring symbols of their reign and achievements.

For young readers, the stories of these Tamil kings and queens offer numerous valuable lessons. They teach us the importance of courage, wisdom, and compassion in leadership. Rajaraja Chola's dedication to learning and justice reminds us that true leadership requires both strength and intellect. Rajendra Chola's open court sessions emphasize the importance of fairness and accessibility in governance. Queen Velu Nachiyar's resilience in the face of adversity shows that determination and strategic thinking can overcome even the most formidable challenges.

These stories also highlight the significance of dreams and determination. From a young prince with aspirations of greatness to a legendary king who built an empire, Rajaraja Chola's journey teaches us that with hard work and perseverance, we can achieve our goals. Queen Velu Nachiyar's fight against colonial forces demonstrates the power of standing up for what is right, even when faced with overwhelming odds.

The tale of these Tamil rulers is not just a recounting of historical events but a celebration of values and principles that resonate across time. They encourage us to be just, kind, and wise in our actions and to strive for excellence in everything we do. By following their example, we can all contribute to building a better and more prosperous world.

As we conclude this introduction, let us embark on this journey through the pages of history, learning from the lives of the Tamil kings and queens who have shaped the rich cultural heritage of Tamil Nadu.

Their stories will inspire us, teach us, and remind us of the enduring power of vision, leadership, and justice.

The Tamil kings and queens left an indelible mark on history through their visionary leadership, dedication to justice, and commitment to cultural and intellectual pursuits. Their reigns were characterized by prosperity, innovation, and a deep sense of responsibility towards their people and the environment. Their stories continue to inspire and offer valuable lessons for future generations.

As we immerse ourselves in their tales, we will discover the timeless values and principles that guided these remarkable rulers. Their legacy is a testament to the power of visionary leadership and the enduring impact of justice, compassion, and innovation in shaping a prosperous and harmonious society.

In conclusion, the stories of the Tamil kings and queens serve as a powerful reminder of the enduring values that have shaped the rich cultural heritage of Tamil Nadu. Their dedication to justice, compassion, innovation, and cultural patronage continues to inspire and guide us today. The grand temples, inscriptions, and artifacts they left behind stand as enduring symbols of their reign and achievements.

As we reflect on their lives and contributions, we are reminded of the importance of visionary leadership and the impact it can have on society. The Tamil rulers understood that true leadership encompassed not only military strength and political acumen but also a deep commitment to the welfare of their people. Their reigns were characterized by a balance of power and compassion, ensuring that their kingdoms thrived both economically and socially.

For young readers, these stories offer numerous valuable lessons. They teach us the importance of courage, wisdom, and compassion in leadership. They inspire us to dream big, work hard, and strive for excellence in everything we do. By following their example, we can all contribute to building a better and more prosperous world.

Let us embark on this journey through the pages of history, learning from the lives of these extraordinary rulers who have shaped the rich cultural heritage of Tamil Nadu. Their tales will inspire us, teach us, and remind us of the enduring power of vision, leadership, and justice.

Chapter Two

THE LEGEND OF KING RAJARAJA CHOLA

Once upon a time, in the land of Southern India, there was a mighty kingdom known as the Chola Empire. It was a land of great wealth, culture, and history. Among the Chola rulers, one name stood out like a shining star - King Rajaraja Chola. But before he became a legendary king, he was known as Arulmozhivarman, a young and curious prince with a heart full of dreams and a mind eager to learn.

Arulmozhivarman was born into a royal family, surrounded by the grandeur of palaces and the wisdom of scholars. From a young age, he showed signs of greatness. He was not only brave and strong but also kind-hearted and wise beyond his years. His father, King Sundara Chola, and his mother, Vanavan Mahadevi, made sure he received the best education. They taught him about the rich history of their land, the importance of justice, and the value of kindness.

As a child, Arulmozhivarman loved exploring the lush gardens of the palace, playing with his friends, and listening to the stories of brave warriors and wise kings. These stories ignited a spark in his heart. He dreamed of becoming a king who would be loved by his people and remembered for his greatness. Little did he know that one day, his dreams would come true, and he would be known as Rajaraja Chola, one of the greatest kings in history.

Arulmozhivarman's childhood was filled with adventures and learning. Every day was a new opportunity to discover something amazing. He would often join his friends in friendly competitions, showing his skills in archery, sword fighting, and horseback riding. Though he was a prince, he never let his royal status make him arrogant. Instead, he was always ready to lend a helping hand and share his knowledge with others.

One of his favorite places in the palace was the library, a vast room filled with scrolls and manuscripts from different parts of the world. He loved to sit there for hours, engrossed in tales of valor and wisdom. The stories of great kings and their heroic deeds fascinated him. His mentor, a wise sister Kundavai, played a significant role in shaping his mind. Kundavai would often tell him, "A true king is not just a warrior but also a scholar. Knowledge is as important as strength."

Arulmozhivarman took these words to heart. He understood that to be a great king, he needed to be knowledgeable, just, and kind. He began to pay more attention to the lessons of history, governance, and the arts. He learned about the importance of agriculture, trade, and building strong relationships with neighboring kingdoms. His parents were proud of his dedication and wisdom, seeing in him the future of their beloved Chola Empire.

As the years passed, Arulmozhivarman grew into a young man of remarkable qualities. He was admired by everyone in the kingdom for his intelligence, bravery, and kindness. However, his journey to kingship was not without challenges. When his father, King Sundara Chola, fell ill, the kingdom faced a time of uncertainty. The question of succession loomed large, and not everyone was in favor of Arul-mozhivarman becoming the next king.

Some members of the royal court believed that his elder brother, Aditya Karikalan, should be the rightful heir. This created tension and rivalry within the palace. Despite these challenges, Arulmozhivar-man remained calm and focused. He knew that a true leader must face adversity with courage and wisdom. He sought counsel from his mother and his sister Kundavai, who advised him to remain patient and continue to prepare himself for the responsibilities of kingship.

Tragedy struck when Aditya Karikalan was mysteriously assassi-nated. The kingdom was plunged into sorrow and confusion. Amidst the turmoil, Arulmozhivarman stepped forward, determined to bring stability and peace to the land. With the support of his mother and the loyal subjects of the kingdom, he ascended to the throne, taking on the name Rajaraja Chola. His coronation was a moment of hope and renewal for the Chola Empire.

As King Rajaraja Chola, he vowed to make his empire the greatest it had ever been. His vision was clear – to build a strong, prosperous, and culturally rich kingdom. He began by strengthening the military and embarking on campaigns to expand the empire's territories. His first major conquest was the capture of the island of Lanka (modern-day Sri Lanka), which brought immense wealth and resources to the Chola Empire.

Rajaraja Chola was not just a conqueror; he was also a builder and a patron of the arts. He believed that a great empire should have magnificent temples, libraries, and schools. He commissioned the construction of the Brihadeeswarar Temple in Thanjavur, a marvel of architecture and a symbol of the Chola Empire's grandeur. The temple, with its towering vimana (tower) and intricate sculptures, became a center of culture and learning.

Under his rule, the Chola Empire flourished in every aspect. He promoted trade with distant lands, establishing connections with Southeast Asia, China, and the Middle East. The ports of the Chola Empire were bustling with activity, welcoming traders from far and wide. Rajaraja Chola's policies encouraged economic growth and ensured that the wealth of the empire was shared among its people.

One of the most remarkable aspects of Rajaraja Chola's reign was his deep sense of justice and compassion. He believed that a king's duty was to serve his people and ensure their well-being. Stories of his kindness and fairness spread throughout the land. He often traveled incognito to understand the lives of his subjects better. Disguised as a commoner, he would visit villages, listen to the grievances of the people, and take swift action to address their concerns.

There was a famous story about how he once visited a village where the farmers were struggling with a severe drought. Rajaraja Chola immediately ordered the construction of a vast network of canals and reservoirs to ensure a steady supply of water. This not only solved the immediate problem but also brought long-term prosperity to the region. The grateful villagers built a small shrine in his honor, calling him the "Savior of the Fields."

Rajaraja Chola's wisdom was evident in his administration. He implemented an efficient system of governance, dividing the empire into manageable provinces, each overseen by trusted officials. He encouraged local self-governance and allowed village councils to make decisions on matters affecting their communities. This approach not only ensured smooth administration but also empowered the people, fostering a sense of responsibility and pride in their roles.

Another significant achievement of Rajaraja Chola was his support for education and the arts. He believed that a cultured and knowledgeable society was the foundation of a strong empire. He established numerous schools and libraries, where scholars could study and share their knowledge. He invited poets, artists, and musicians to his court, encouraging them to create works that would inspire and educate future generations.

The Brihadeeswarar Temple, apart from being a religious center, also became a hub of learning and artistic expression. It housed a vast collection of manuscripts and served as a venue for cultural performances. Rajaraja Chola's patronage of the arts led to a renaissance in literature, music, and dance. The Chola bronze sculptures, depicting deities and mythological scenes, became renowned for their beauty and craftsmanship.

Rajaraja Chola's contributions to art and culture had a lasting impact, influencing not only his kingdom but also neighboring regions. The Chola style of architecture and sculpture set a standard that was admired and emulated by other kingdoms. His reign marked a golden age for the Chola Empire, where prosperity and cultural richness went hand in hand.

Despite his achievements, Rajaraja Chola never lost sight of the challenges and responsibilities that came with his position. He knew that being a king was not just about glory and power but also about making difficult decisions for the greater good. One such challenge came in the form of conflicts with neighboring kingdoms and internal dissent.

Rajaraja Chola faced these challenges with a combination of strength and diplomacy. He believed in maintaining peace through strong alliances and treaties. He married his daughters into the royal families of neighboring kingdoms, forging bonds that helped prevent conflicts. When conflicts did arise, he was always ready to lead his army into battle, demonstrating his courage and strategic acumen.

His most significant military campaign was against the Western Chalukyas, a powerful kingdom to the north. The campaign was long and arduous, but Rajaraja Chola's leadership and the loyalty of his generals and soldiers ensured victory. The defeat of the Western Chalukyas secured the northern borders of the Chola Empire and brought new territories under its control.

Rajaraja Chola's leadership extended beyond the battlefield. He was also a skilled administrator who introduced several innovations in governance. He implemented a systematic method of land revenue assessment and collection, ensuring that the empire's wealth was used effectively for the development of infrastructure and public services. This system provided a stable source of income for the kingdom and helped in the construction of roads, canals, and temples.

He also paid special attention to the welfare of his soldiers and their families. Understanding the sacrifices made by his warriors, he ensured that they were well-compensated and their families taken care of. He established a system of pensions for retired soldiers and provided land grants to those who had served the kingdom loyally. This policy not only secured the loyalty of his army but also promoted a sense of honor and duty among the soldiers.

The administrative reforms introduced by Rajaraja Chola laid the foundation for a well-organized and prosperous empire. His efficient governance ensured that the people of the Chola Empire enjoyed peace, stability, and prosperity. His reign became a model for future generations of rulers, both within the Chola dynasty and beyond.

Rajaraja Chola's relations with other kingdoms were characterized by a blend of diplomacy and strength. He understood the importance of maintaining peaceful and cooperative relationships with neighboring rulers. Through strategic marriages, treaties, and alliances, he ensured that the Chola Empire remained secure and influential in the region.

One of his notable diplomatic achievements was establishing strong ties with the kingdoms of Southeast Asia. The Chola navy, renowned for its strength and efficiency, played a crucial role in these diplomatic efforts. The navy not only protected the empire's maritime interests but also facilitated trade and cultural exchanges with distant lands. Rajaraja Chola's policies encouraged merchants to venture far and wide, bringing back wealth and exotic goods that enriched the Chola Empire.

The cultural and economic exchanges with Southeast Asia had a profound impact on both regions. The influence of Chola art, architecture, and culture spread to countries like Cambodia, Thailand, and Indonesia. Temples and monuments inspired by Chola architecture can still be seen in these regions today, a testament to the lasting legacy of Rajaraja Chola's reign.

Amidst his numerous responsibilities, Rajaraja Chola never forgot his people. He often held public audiences where his subjects could present their grievances and seek justice. He listened attentively, showing genuine concern for their problems. His fairness and willingness to help earned him the love and respect of his people. They saw him not just as a ruler but as a guardian and protector.

One story that highlights his kindness involves a dispute between two farmers over a piece of land. Rajaraja Chola personally visited the disputed land and spoke to both parties. After carefully considering their arguments, he made a fair decision that satisfied both farmers. His hands-on approach to governance and his ability to empathize with his subjects made him a beloved ruler.

Rajaraja Chola's reign was marked by a series of wise and just decisions that benefited the empire and its people. His policies promoted economic growth, social harmony, and cultural development. He believed that the true measure of a king's success was the happiness and prosperity of his subjects. Under his rule, the Chola Empire became a beacon of justice and fairness, admired by all who knew of it.

As the years went by, Rajaraja Chola continued to build on his successes. He remained dedicated to his vision of a strong and prosperous empire. His tireless efforts ensured that the Chola Empire reached new heights of glory. The legacy of his reign was not just in the magnificent structures he built or the territories he conquered but also in the values he upheld.

Rajaraja Chola's impact extended beyond his lifetime. His son, Rajendra Chola, inherited a powerful and well-organized empire. Inspired by his father's example, Rajendra Chola continued the legacy of expansion and cultural patronage. He embarked on ambitious military campaigns, including a remarkable naval expedition to Southeast Asia, further solidifying the Chola Empire's dominance in the region.

The foundations laid by Rajaraja Chola ensured that the empire remained strong and influential for generations. His contributions to art, culture, and governance left an indelible mark on history. The temples he built, the policies he implemented, and the stories of his kindness and wisdom continued to inspire future generations of rulers and subjects alike.

For young readers, the story of Rajaraja Chola offers many valuable lessons. His life teaches us the importance of courage, wisdom, and compassion. Rajaraja Chola's dedication to learning and his respect for knowledge remind us that true leadership requires both strength and intellect. His fair and just rule shows us that kindness and empathy are essential qualities for any leader.

Rajaraja Chola's story also highlights the significance of dreams and determination. From a young prince with dreams of greatness, he grew into a legendary king who transformed his vision into reality. His journey teaches us that with hard work, perseverance, and a clear vision, we can achieve our goals and make a positive impact on the world.

The tale of Rajaraja Chola is not just a story of a king and his empire; it is a story of values and principles that resonate across time. It encourages us to be just, kind, and wise in our actions, and to strive for excellence in everything we do. By following the example of Rajaraja Chola, we can all contribute to building a better and more prosperous world.

The end of Rajaraja Chola's reign marked the beginning of a new chapter for the Chola Empire. His achievements set a high standard for future rulers. His son, Rajendra Chola, carried forward his father's legacy, expanding the empire and enhancing its cultural and economic stature. Under Rajendra's rule, the Chola Empire continued to thrive, reaching even greater heights.

Rajaraja Chola's story continued to be told through generations, not just in the Chola Empire but also in distant lands. His legacy was immortalized in the temples he built, the inscriptions he left behind, and the stories passed down by storytellers. The Brihadeeswarar Temple, in particular, stood as a testament to his vision and greatness. Its towering structure and intricate carvings became symbols of the Chola Empire's architectural brilliance.

As time passed, the Chola Empire eventually declined, but the memory of Rajaraja Chola endured. His reign became a golden era that future generations looked back upon with admiration and pride. Historians and scholars studied his life and contributions, ensuring that his legacy would never be forgotten.

Today, the story of Rajaraja Chola continues to inspire people of all ages. For children, it is a tale of bravery, wisdom, and kindness. It teaches them that true greatness comes from within and that the most important qualities of a leader are compassion and justice. Rajaraja Chola's life reminds us that every challenge can be overcome with determination and the right mindset.

Modern historians and archaeologists continue to uncover new insights into his reign, shedding light on his achievements and the impact of his policies. The temples and monuments he built are now cherished heritage sites, visited by people from all over the world. They stand as a reminder of the rich cultural heritage of the Chola Empire and the remarkable legacy of Rajaraja Chola.

As we look back on his life, we are reminded of the enduring values that he championed. Rajaraja Chola's story is a celebration of human potential and the power of vision and leadership. It encourages us to aspire to greatness and to lead with wisdom and compassion, just as he did.

The legend of Rajaraja Chola is a story of a remarkable king who transformed his dreams into reality. From a young prince with a thirst for knowledge to a legendary ruler who built a magnificent empire, his life is an inspiration to all. Rajaraja Chola's contributions to art, culture, and governance have left an indelible mark on history, and his legacy continues to inspire generations.

As children read about his adventures and achievements, they learn valuable lessons about courage, wisdom, and kindness. They discover that true leadership is not just about power but also about serving others and making a positive impact on the world. The story of Rajaraja Chola reminds us all that with vision, determination, and a heart full of compassion, we can achieve greatness and create a better future for ourselves and others.

CHAPTER THREE

THE BRAVE QUEEN VELU NACHIYAR

Once upon a time, in a land rich with culture and history, there was a kingdom named Sivaganga in southern India. This kingdom was known for its prosperity, vibrant traditions, and brave rulers. Among these rulers was a remarkable queen who would go down in history as one of the bravest and most intelligent leaders. Her name was Velu Nachiyar.

Velu Nachiyar was born in 1730 to the royal family of Ramnad. She was the cherished daughter of King Chellamuthu Vijayaragunatha Sethupathy and Queen Sakandimuthal. From a young age, it was clear that Velu Nachiyar was no ordinary princess. She was curious, intelligent, and eager to learn everything she could about the world around her.

Unlike many princesses of her time, Velu Nachiyar was trained in the art of warfare. She learned to wield a sword with skill, ride horses with grace, and strategize like a seasoned general. Her parents ensured that she received the best education possible, not only in combat but also in languages, including English, French, and Urdu. This extensive training prepared her for the challenging path that lay ahead.

As Velu Nachiyar grew older, her intelligence and bravery became even more apparent. She married Muthu Vaduganatha Periya Udaiyathevar, the prince of Sivaganga, and together, they ruled the kingdom with wisdom and compassion. The people of Sivaganga adored their queen, not just for her noble birth but for her genuine care and leadership.

But life in the kingdom was not always peaceful. During this time, the British East India Company was expanding its control over India, and their eyes were set on Sivaganga. The British were known for their cunning tactics and superior weaponry, which made them a formidable enemy.

One fateful day, the British launched an attack on Sivaganga. The battle was fierce and devastating. Despite the valiant efforts of the king and his warriors, the British forces proved too powerful. In the chaos of the battle, Velu Nachiyar's beloved husband was killed, and the kingdom was lost to the British.

Heartbroken but undeterred, Velu Nachiyar knew she had to fight back. She could not let the British conquer her homeland and subjugate her people. With a heavy heart but a determined spirit, she fled the kingdom to regroup and plan her next move. Velu Nachiyar sought refuge with her allies and began the arduous task of gathering support to reclaim her throne.

During her time in exile, Velu Nachiyar did not remain idle. She traveled extensively, seeking allies and building a coalition to challenge the British. She forged alliances with other rulers and powerful leaders who shared her vision of a free and independent Sivaganga. Her intelligence and diplomatic skills were crucial in gaining the trust and support of these allies.

While in exile, Velu Nachiyar trained tirelessly, honing her combat skills and preparing herself for the battles to come. She knew that reclaiming her kingdom would not be easy, but she was determined to fight for her people and restore their freedom. Her unwavering resolve and courage inspired those around her, and her loyal supporters grew in number.

As she gathered her forces, Velu Nachiyar carefully planned her strategy. She knew that brute strength alone would not be enough to defeat the British; she needed to outsmart them. Her keen intellect and deep understanding of military tactics allowed her to devise innovative strategies that would give her an edge in battle.

One of her most brilliant strategies was to use guerilla warfare tactics. Velu Nachiyar knew that a direct confrontation with the well-equipped British army would be disastrous. Instead, she opted for surprise attacks and ambushes, using the terrain to her advantage. Her knowledge of the local landscape and her ability to think on her feet made her a formidable opponent.

Velu Nachiyar's leadership and bravery soon became legendary. Stories of her daring exploits spread far and wide, inspiring others to join her cause. Her ability to inspire and lead her people was a testament to her strength and character. She was not just a queen; she was a warrior and a beacon of hope for her people.

One of the most remarkable aspects of Velu Nachiyar's leadership was her ability to rally her people around a common cause. She instilled a sense of pride and purpose in her followers, reminding them of their rich heritage and the importance of fighting for their freedom. Her speeches were filled with passion and conviction, and her words resonated deeply with her people.

Among her loyal supporters were several key figures who played crucial roles in her campaign. One such figure was Kuyili, a fearless woman who became one of Velu Nachiyar's closest confidantes and trusted generals. Kuyili's bravery and loyalty were unmatched, and she was instrumental in many of the queen's military successes.

Another important ally was Marudhu Brothers, Periya Marudhu and Chinna Marudhu, who were known for their exceptional combat skills and strategic acumen. They provided invaluable support to Velu Nachiyar, both on and off the battlefield. Together, they formed a formidable team that posed a significant threat to the British forces.

As Velu Nachiyar's army grew in strength and numbers, the time came to launch a full-scale assault on the British-held Sivaganga. The queen and her allies meticulously planned their attack, taking into account every possible scenario. They knew that this battle would be a turning point in their struggle for freedom.

The day of the battle arrived, and the atmosphere was charged with anticipation and determination. Velu Nachiyar, clad in her warrior attire, led her troops with unwavering confidence. Her presence on the battlefield was electrifying, and her soldiers drew immense strength from her courage and resolve.

The battle was intense and hard-fought. The British, taken by surprise by Velu Nachiyar's guerilla tactics, struggled to maintain their ground. The queen and her forces attacked from all sides, using the element of surprise to their advantage. Velu Nachiyar herself fought at the forefront, displaying remarkable skill and bravery.

In the midst of the chaos, Velu Nachiyar devised a plan to target the British ammunition depot. She knew that disabling their supply of weapons and ammunition would significantly weaken their forces. Kuyili, her trusted general, volunteered for the dangerous mission. Disguised as a British soldier, Kuyili infiltrated the depot and set it ablaze, causing a massive explosion that crippled the British forces.

This decisive move turned the tide of the battle in Velu Nachiyar's favor. With their ammunition supply destroyed and their morale shattered, the British troops began to retreat. The queen and her army pursued them relentlessly, driving them out of Sivaganga. The victory was a testament to Velu Nachiyar's strategic brilliance and indomitable spirit.

With the British forces in retreat, Velu Nachiyar wasted no time in securing her kingdom. She immediately set about restoring order and rebuilding what had been destroyed during the conflict. Her first priority was to ensure the safety and well-being of her people. She implemented measures to provide food, shelter, and medical care to those affected by the war.

The people of Sivaganga rejoiced at the return of their beloved queen. They celebrated her victory with grand festivities, honoring her bravery and leadership. Velu Nachiyar's triumph was not just a personal victory but a symbol of hope and resilience for all who had suffered under British rule.

Velu Nachiyar's success did not go unnoticed. Her victory against the British earned her widespread acclaim and respect. Other rulers and leaders across India were inspired by her courage and determination. She became a symbol of resistance against colonial oppression, and her story was passed down through generations as a beacon of hope.

Despite the challenges she faced, Velu Nachiyar remained humble and focused on her mission. She continued to lead her people with wisdom and compassion, ensuring that her kingdom prospered once again. Her reign was marked by peace, stability, and progress, and she left an indelible mark on the history of Sivaganga.

As the years went by, Velu Nachiyar's legacy grew stronger. She became a legend, not just in Sivaganga but throughout India. Her story of bravery, intelligence, and unwavering determination inspired countless others to stand up against injustice and fight for their rights.

Velu Nachiyar's leadership extended beyond the battlefield. She was a visionary ruler who implemented numerous reforms to improve the lives of her people. She promoted education, encouraged cultural and artistic endeavors, and worked tirelessly to uplift the marginalized sections of society. Her efforts to empower women were particularly noteworthy, as she believed in their potential to contribute to the progress of the kingdom.

One of her significant contributions was the establishment of schools and centers for learning. Velu Nachiyar understood the importance of education in shaping the future of her kingdom. She ensured that children, especially girls, had access to quality education. Her emphasis on education and knowledge helped lay the foundation for a more enlightened and progressive society.

Velu Nachiyar's reign also saw the flourishing of arts and culture. She patronized artists, musicians, and scholars, creating an environment where creativity thrived. The kingdom of Sivaganga became a hub of cultural activities, attracting talents from far and wide. This cultural renaissance added to the glory of her rule and left a lasting legacy.

As Velu Nachiyar continued to lead her kingdom, she remained vigilant against any threats to its sovereignty. She maintained a strong and disciplined army, always ready to defend Sivaganga from external aggressors. Her strategic alliances with neighboring kingdoms ensured a network of support and cooperation that further strengthened her position.

One of the most inspiring aspects of Velu Nachiyar's reign was her deep connection with her people. She was not just a ruler but a beloved figure who genuinely cared for the well-being of her subjects. She often traveled throughout her kingdom, listening to the concerns of her people and addressing their needs. Her approachable and compassionate nature earned her the love and respect of her citizens.

Velu Nachiyar's story is a testament to the power of resilience and determination. She faced immense challenges, from the loss of her husband and kingdom to the constant threat of British invasion. Yet, she never wavered in her commitment to her people and her land. Her courage and intelligence guided her through the darkest times, leading her to victory and restoration.

Her legacy continues to inspire generations. Velu Nachiyar is remembered as a warrior queen who stood up against colonial rule and fought for her people's freedom. Her story is a reminder that even in the face of overwhelming odds, bravery and intelligence can prevail.

In the annals of history, Velu Nachiyar's name is etched as a symbol of strength and perseverance. Her story is often told to children, not just in Sivaganga but across India, as a source of inspiration and pride. Her life serves as a powerful reminder of the importance of standing up for what is right and just.

Velu Nachiyar's impact extended beyond her lifetime. She paved the way for future generations of leaders, particularly women, to rise and take their rightful place in society. Her example showed that women could be formidable warriors and wise rulers, capable of leading with both strength and compassion.

As we reflect on the life of Velu Nachiyar, it is important to recognize the values she embodied: bravery, intelligence, and an unwavering commitment to her people. These values are timeless and continue to resonate with us today. Her story teaches us that true leadership is about service, sacrifice, and the relentless pursuit of justice.

For young readers, Velu Nachiyar's tale is a captivating adventure filled with lessons about courage and resilience. It encourages them to dream big, to stand up for what they believe in, and to never give up, no matter how difficult the journey may be. Her legacy is a beacon of hope and inspiration for all.

Velu Nachiyar's reign eventually came to an end, but her legacy lived on through the stories and legends passed down through generations. The people of Sivaganga continued to honor her memory, celebrating her contributions and remembering the sacrifices she made for their freedom.

In the years that followed, Sivaganga flourished under the leadership of those who were inspired by Velu Nachiyar's example. Her emphasis on education, cultural enrichment, and social welfare laid the groundwork for a prosperous and enlightened society. The principles she championed continued to guide the kingdom, ensuring that her vision of a just and thriving Sivaganga endured.

Today, Velu Nachiyar's story is celebrated in various forms. Statues and monuments have been erected in her honor, and her life is depicted in books, plays, and films. Schools and institutions are named after her, keeping her legacy alive and inspiring new generations to learn about her extraordinary life.

Velu Nachiyar's tale is not just a chapter in history but a source of inspiration that transcends time and place. Her bravery, intelligence, and unwavering dedication to her people serve as a powerful reminder of what one person can achieve when driven by a sense of justice and purpose.

Let us remember Velu Nachiyar not just as a warrior queen but as a beacon of hope and resilience. Her story will continue to inspire and motivate us to face our challenges with courage and determination, just as she did.

Chapter Four

THE MIGHTY KING KARIKALA CHOLA

In the ancient lands of Tamil Nadu, nestled along the banks of the mighty Kaveri River, lived a wise and benevolent ruler named King Karikala Chola. His kingdom was a place of rich culture and prosperity, where the Tamil language and arts flourished. But despite its many blessings, the kingdom faced a significant challenge: the unpredictable and often scarce supply of water. This was a time long before modern technology, and the people depended heavily on the rivers for their agriculture and daily needs.

King Karikala Chola, known for his keen intellect and deep care for his subjects, observed the struggles of his people with great concern. The farmers toiled under the harsh sun, praying for rains that sometimes never came. The once fertile lands often lay parched and cracked, leading to poor harvests and hunger. Karikala knew that without a reliable water source, his beloved kingdom could not thrive as it should.

One evening, as the king walked along the banks of the Kaveri River, an idea began to take shape in his mind. He envisioned a grand structure that could harness the power of the river, ensuring a steady and reliable supply of water for his people. This vision marked the beginning of an extraordinary journey, one that would change the fate of his kingdom forever.

Karikala's vision was ambitious, but he was not a man to shy away from challenges. He called upon his most trusted advisors, engineers, and wise men to discuss his plan. "We need a solution that will bring water to our lands throughout the year," he declared. The idea of building a dam was met with both excitement and skepticism. Some feared it would be an impossible feat, but Karikala's determination was unwavering.

The king led by example, involving himself deeply in the planning and design phase. He spent countless hours with the engineers, discussing every detail and overcoming the doubts of those who thought it could not be done. The location was carefully chosen along the Kaveri River, where the natural landscape would support such a grand construction. Plans were drawn up for a massive stone dam that would be strong enough to withstand the river's powerful currents and last for generations.

As news of the king's plan spread, the people of the kingdom began to feel a spark of hope. They admired their king's dedication to their well-being and were inspired to support him in any way they could. The entire community came together, each person ready to contribute their skills and labor to the monumental project.

The construction of the Kallanai Dam, as it came to be known, was a truly collaborative effort. Men and women from all walks of life joined hands, working tirelessly day and night. The king himself could often be seen at the construction site, encouraging the workers and offering his assistance wherever it was needed. His presence and unwavering spirit kept morale high, even during the most challenging times.

Building the dam was no easy task. The workers faced numerous obstacles, from the unforgiving heat to the ever-present threat of floods. Yet, they persevered, driven by the vision of a prosperous future. They used massive stones, each carefully cut and placed, to form the foundation of the dam. Ingenious techniques were employed to ensure the structure's strength and stability, showcasing the advanced engineering skills of the time.

As the dam began to take shape, the sense of unity and purpose among the people grew stronger. They shared stories and songs, encouraging one another through the long days of labor. Families brought food and water to the workers, and children played nearby, their laughter a testament to the hope and joy that the project had brought to the community. The dream of a bountiful and secure kingdom was coming closer to reality with each passing day.

After many months of relentless effort, the day finally arrived when the last stone was set in place. The Kallanai Dam stood tall and proud, a testament to the ingenuity and determination of King Karikala Chola and his people. A grand celebration was held to mark this monumental achievement, with festivities that lasted for several days. The air was filled with the sounds of music and laughter as the entire kingdom came together to honor their shared success.

King Karikala Chola stood before his people, his heart swelling with pride and gratitude. "This dam is not just a structure of stone," he proclaimed, "but a symbol of our unity and resilience. It will provide for us and for generations to come." The crowd erupted in cheers, their voices echoing across the valley.

The impact of the Kallanai Dam was immediate and profound. The once dry and barren fields now glistened with life as water flowed steadily through the irrigation channels. Crops flourished, and the people enjoyed bountiful harvests. The kingdom's prosperity soared, and the fear of drought became a distant memory. The dam had transformed their lives, bringing security and hope to every corner of the realm.

With the Kallanai Dam in place, the people of Tamil Nadu experienced a golden age of abundance and happiness. The steady supply of water allowed farmers to cultivate their lands more effectively, leading to an increase in crop diversity and yields. Fruits, vegetables, and grains thrived, and the markets overflowed with fresh produce. The kingdom became a hub of trade, attracting merchants from far and wide who marveled at the fertile lands and the ingenuity of its people.

King Karikala Chola continued to oversee the maintenance and improvement of the dam, ensuring that it remained in perfect condition. He appointed skilled engineers to monitor the structure and make any necessary adjustments. The dam was more than just an engineering marvel; it was a living, breathing part of the kingdom, cared for and cherished by all.

The king's dedication to his people did not go unnoticed. Stories of his wisdom and compassion spread far and wide, and neighboring kingdoms sent envoys to learn from his success. Karikala welcomed them with open arms, eager to share the knowledge and experience that had brought such prosperity to his land. His reign was marked by peace and cooperation, as he fostered strong relationships with other rulers and worked towards a brighter future for all.

Despite his many achievements, King Karikala Chola remained humble and ever mindful of his responsibilities. He often traveled through the kingdom, speaking with his subjects and listening to their concerns. His genuine care for their well-being endeared him to all, and the people loved him as both a leader and a father figure. He believed that the true measure of a king's success was not in grand monuments, but in the happiness and prosperity of his people.

As years passed, the Kallanai Dam continued to serve as a lifeline for the kingdom. It became a source of inspiration and pride, reminding everyone of what could be achieved through unity and determination. The children of the kingdom grew up hearing tales of their mighty king and the great dam he had built, dreaming of contributing to their land's legacy in their own ways.

One day, as Karikala stood by the dam, he reflected on the journey that had brought him and his people to this point. The struggles and triumphs had forged a bond that could never be broken. He knew that the future held many more challenges, but he was confident that his kingdom was prepared to face them. Together, they had transformed a dream into reality, and their story would inspire generations to come.

In the twilight of his reign, King Karikala Chola looked upon his kingdom with a sense of fulfillment. The Kallanai Dam was more than just a feat of engineering; it was a testament to the enduring spirit of his people. The lush, green fields and thriving villages were a daily reminder of their collective strength and resilience. Karikala's heart swelled with pride each time he saw the fruits of their labor.

The dam not only provided water for agriculture but also played a crucial role in flood control. During the monsoon seasons, the structure helped regulate the river's flow, preventing devastating floods that had once plagued the region. This newfound stability allowed the kingdom to flourish in ways that had previously seemed impossible. The people lived without fear of nature's unpredictability, knowing that they had the means to protect and sustain their way of life.

As the years went by, the Kallanai Dam became a symbol of innovation and forward-thinking. Scholars and engineers from distant lands traveled to study its construction, eager to learn from the brilliance of King Karikala Chola's vision. The knowledge shared with these visitors sparked new ideas and projects in their own regions, spreading the spirit of progress and cooperation far beyond the borders of Tamil Nadu.

King Karikala Chola's legacy extended beyond the physical structure of the Kallanai Dam. He had instilled in his people a deep appreciation for ingenuity and a commitment to the greater good. This ethos permeated every aspect of life in the kingdom, from education to governance. Schools and academies flourished, teaching not only traditional subjects but also the values of collaboration and perseverance that had brought about the dam's success.

The king's emphasis on education and innovation bore fruit in unexpected ways. Young minds, inspired by the story of the dam, began to explore new fields of study. They delved into mathematics, astronomy, medicine, and the arts, contributing to a vibrant culture of learning and discovery. The kingdom became a beacon of knowledge, attracting scholars and thinkers from all corners of the world.

Karikala's reign also saw the establishment of numerous public works projects. Roads, bridges, and public buildings were constructed with the same dedication to excellence that had characterized the dam's construction. Each project was a reflection of the king's belief in the importance of serving the people and improving their lives. His administration was marked by transparency and accountability, setting a standard for future generations of leaders.

The influence of King Karikala Chola and the Kallanai Dam reached far beyond the borders of his kingdom. Other rulers and leaders, inspired by his achievements, sought to implement similar projects in their own lands. They realized that the key to prosperity lay in harnessing natural resources and investing in the well-being of their people. The story of Karikala and the Kallanai Dam became a legend, a tale of vision and perseverance that resonated with all who heard it.

As the years passed, the dam continued to stand strong, a testament to the enduring legacy of its creator. The techniques and principles used in its construction were passed down through generations, forming the foundation for future advancements in engineering and water management. The wisdom of Karikala Chola became a guiding light for those who sought to build a better world.

King Karikala Chola's life and achievements were immortalized in songs, poems, and stories. Bards and storytellers traveled from village to village, recounting the tale of the mighty king who had transformed his kingdom with his vision and determination. These stories captivated the hearts and minds of young and old alike, instilling a sense of pride and inspiration in every listener.

In every corner of the kingdom, the name of King Karikala Chola was spoken with reverence and admiration. His story was not just one of a ruler, but of a man who had dedicated his life to the service of his people. The Kallanai Dam stood as a symbol of his commitment to their welfare, a tangible reminder of what could be achieved through unity and hard work.

The king's efforts also fostered a sense of environmental stewardship among his people. They learned to respect and care for the natural resources that sustained their lives. The practices of sustainable agriculture and water management became ingrained in the culture, ensuring that the benefits of the dam would be enjoyed for generations to come. The land flourished under their care, a living testament to the wisdom of their beloved king.

As Karikala grew older, he began to prepare for the future. He ensured that his successor would carry forward the principles and values that had defined his reign. The transition of power was smooth and peaceful, a reflection of the stability and unity he had cultivated throughout his rule. The new generation of leaders, inspired by his example, continued to build on the foundation he had laid.

The story of King Karikala Chola and the Kallanai Dam continued to inspire long after his reign had ended. The dam itself became a place of pilgrimage for those who wished to see the marvel of engineering and the symbol of human determination. Visitors marveled at the ingenuity and skill that had gone into its construction, and they left with a deeper appreciation for the legacy of the great king.

In the years that followed, the region experienced continued growth and prosperity. The principles of collaboration and innovation that Karikala had championed became the bedrock of the kingdom's development. New projects were undertaken, each building on the successes of the past. The people thrived, secure in the knowledge that their leaders were committed to their well-being and progress.

King Karikala Chola's memory was honored in many ways. Statues and monuments were erected in his name, and his story was taught in schools as an example of visionary leadership. Festivals celebrating his achievements became annual events, drawing people together to remember and celebrate their shared heritage. The king's legacy was woven into the very fabric of the kingdom, a source of pride and inspiration for all.

As time went on, the story of King Karikala Chola and the Kallanai Dam spread beyond the borders of Tamil Nadu. Scholars and historians from different parts of the world documented his achievements, ensuring that his contributions would be remembered and studied for generations to come. The principles he had championed – innovation, unity, and a deep care for the people – resonated with leaders and thinkers across cultures.

The Kallanai Dam itself continued to function as a vital part of the region's infrastructure. Regular maintenance and care ensured that it remained strong and effective, serving as a model for other water management projects. The techniques and strategies employed in its construction influenced the development of similar projects in other parts of the world, showcasing the far-reaching impact of Karikala's vision.

In the hearts and minds of the people, King Karikala Chola remained a beloved figure. His life and legacy were celebrated not just for his achievements, but for the values he embodied. He was remembered as a king who had not only transformed his kingdom but had also inspired countless others to strive for greatness. The story of the mighty king and his remarkable dam became a timeless tale of vision, perseverance, and the enduring power of collective effort.

King Karikala Chola's story continued to inspire new generations. Children grew up hearing tales of his wisdom and bravery, imagining themselves as future leaders who could make a difference in their world. The schools and academies established during his reign flourished, nurturing young minds and fostering a spirit of curiosity and innovation. These institutions became centers of excellence, attracting students from far and wide who were eager to learn and contribute to their communities.

The principles of water management and sustainable agriculture that had been championed by Karikala became integral parts of the educational curriculum. Students learned not only the technical skills needed to build and maintain such projects but also the values of collaboration and stewardship that had made the Kallanai Dam possible. This holistic approach to education ensured that the legacy of King Karikala Chola lived on in the hearts and minds of the people.

Community leaders and elders continued to share stories of the great king, ensuring that his memory remained a vital part of the cultural heritage. Festivals and celebrations were held in his honor, bringing people together to reflect on the past and look forward to the future. The spirit of unity and resilience that had defined Karikala's reign became a guiding light for the kingdom, inspiring all who called it home.

King Karikala Chola's impact was felt far beyond his own lifetime. His vision and leadership set a standard for future generations, guiding them towards a path of sustainable development and collective prosperity. The Kallanai Dam, a masterpiece of engineering, stood as a lasting tribute to his ingenuity and dedication. It continued to provide water and stability to the region, ensuring that the land remained fertile and the people well-nourished.

The king's emphasis on community involvement and shared responsibility left a lasting mark on the kingdom's culture. People understood that they were all part of a greater whole, and that their contributions, no matter how small, played a vital role in the well-being of the entire community. This sense of unity and cooperation became a defining characteristic of Tamil Nadu, influencing how people approached challenges and opportunities alike.

King Karikala Chola's reign was also marked by a spirit of inclusivity and respect for diversity. He recognized the value of different perspectives and encouraged the sharing of knowledge and ideas. This openness to learning and collaboration enriched the kingdom and helped it to thrive in a rapidly changing world. His legacy was a testament to the power of visionary leadership and the enduring strength of a united people.

As the years turned into centuries, the story of King Karikala Chola and the Kallanai Dam remained a cherished part of the cultural heritage of Tamil Nadu. The lessons learned from his reign continued to guide the people, reminding them of the importance of vision, perseverance, and community. The dam itself, standing strong against the test of time, became a symbol of what could be achieved through collective effort and dedication.

Generations of leaders drew inspiration from Karikala's example, striving to emulate his commitment to the well-being of his people. They understood that true greatness lay not in personal glory, but in the positive impact they could make on the lives of others. This legacy of selfless leadership and innovation became a cornerstone of the kingdom's identity, shaping its future for the better.

The story of King Karikala Chola and the Kallanai Dam was passed down through the ages, a beacon of hope and inspiration. It reminded everyone that no challenge was insurmountable when faced with unity and determination. The mighty king's vision and the enduring strength of his people continued to inspire new generations, ensuring that the legacy of the Kallanai Dam would live on forever.

CHAPTER FIVE

THE WISE QUEEN MANGAMMAL

In the ancient kingdom of Madurai, nestled in the heart of southern India, there once lived a queen whose wisdom and fairness were legendary. Her name was Mangammal, and she ruled with a heart full of love for her people and a mind sharp with knowledge. The kingdom of Madurai was a vibrant land, filled with lush green fields, majestic temples, and bustling markets. The people of Madurai were known for their hard work and devotion to their gods, and they looked to their rulers to guide them with kindness and strength.

Mangammal was born into a noble family, the daughter of Tupakula Lingama Nayaka, a respected general in the Madurai kingdom. From a young age, she was taught the importance of wisdom, courage, and fairness. These lessons would shape her into the remarkable leader she would one day become. As she grew older, Mangammal married Chokkanatha Nayak, the ruler of Madurai. Together, they had a son named Rangakrishna Muthu Virappa Nayak. Life seemed perfect, but fate had different plans for Mangammal.

When her husband died in 1682, Mangammal's life took a dramatic turn. Her son became the new ruler, but his reign was short-lived.

After his untimely death in 1689, Mangammal's daughter-in-law, who was pregnant at the time, committed sati, a tragic custom where a widow immolates herself on her husband's funeral pyre. Mangammal was left to care for her young grandson, Vijaya Ranga Chokkanatha, who was too young to rule. Thus, Mangammal became the regent, a position she embraced with determination and compassion.

As the regent, Mangammal faced numerous challenges. The kingdom was in turmoil, and the people were in need of a strong leader to guide them through difficult times. Mangammal rose to the occasion, demonstrating her exceptional administrative skills and unwavering dedication to her people. One of her first tasks was to improve the kingdom's infrastructure. She understood that for a kingdom to prosper, it needed strong foundations, both literally and metaphorically.

Mangammal initiated the construction of new roads, which not only made travel easier but also boosted trade and commerce. She ordered the planting of avenue trees along these roads, providing shade for travelers and enhancing the beauty of the kingdom. Her efforts in improving irrigation channels ensured that farmers had a reliable water supply, leading to bountiful harvests and a flourishing agrarian economy.

The queen's love for her subjects was evident in every decision she made. She built temples, tanks, and choultries (rest houses) for the benefit of her people. One of her most notable projects was the construction of the "Spring Palace" at TumKum (Thamukkam), a beautiful retreat that showcased her architectural vision. This palace later became the Gandhi Memorial Museum in Madurai, a testament to her lasting legacy.

Mangammal's reign was not just about physical improvements; she also focused on the well-being of her people. She implemented fair policies, ensuring that justice was accessible to all, regardless of their social status. Her court was known for its impartiality, and she gained the respect and admiration of her subjects.

One of the most remarkable aspects of Queen Mangammal's rule was her diplomatic acumen. She knew that maintaining peace and forging strong alliances were crucial for the stability of her kingdom. Mangammal was a master negotiator, and her diplomatic skills were put to the test when she had to deal with the powerful Mughal Empire.

During her regency, the Mughal Emperor Aurangzeb sought to expand his empire, and southern India was in his sights. Mangammal recognized the threat but also saw an opportunity. She decided to acknowledge Aurangzeb as her suzerain, a strategic move that allowed her to maintain a degree of autonomy while gaining the support of the Mughal army. This alliance proved beneficial when the kingdom faced the Siege of Jinji.

The Siege of Jinji was a significant military campaign in which Mangammal played a key role. Rajaram, a renegade who opposed the Mughal rule, had fortified himself within the Jinji fort and posed a threat to Thanjavur and Madurai. Mangammal, understanding the importance of unity against common enemies, collaborated with Zulfiqar Khan, the Mughal general, to capture the fort. After an arduous eight-year siege, the fort fell, and peace was restored to the region. This victory not only secured Madurai's safety but also strengthened Mangammal's position as a capable and astute leader.

Mangammal's military achievements were matched by her contributions to the cultural and spiritual life of her kingdom. She was a great patron of the arts, and under her rule, Madurai flourished as a center of culture and learning. She supported poets, artists, and scholars, creating an environment where creativity and knowledge could thrive. Festivals and celebrations became grander, bringing joy and a sense of unity among her people.

One of the most cherished festivals introduced by Mangammal was the Unjal festival at the Meenakshi Temple during the Tamil month of Ahni. This festival saw the royal families and citizens gather to pay tribute to Meenakshi Amman, the goddess of the temple. The festivities were a time of music, dance, and community, reflecting Mangammal's dedication to preserving and enhancing the cultural heritage of her kingdom.

Mangammal's reign was also marked by her deep respect for religious diversity. She built and restored many temples, ensuring that places of worship were well-maintained and accessible to all. Her efforts in constructing tanks and choultries provided pilgrims with essential amenities, making religious journeys more comfortable and inviting.

Despite her many successes, Mangammal's rule was not without its challenges. Internal strife and external threats constantly tested her leadership. Yet, she remained steadfast, always prioritizing the welfare of her kingdom and its people. Her ability to navigate these difficulties with grace and determination solidified her reputation as one of the wisest and most beloved rulers of Madurai.

As the years passed, Mangammal's grandson, Vijaya Ranga Chokkanatha, grew older. By 1704, he was of age to take over the reins of the kingdom. However, Mangammal and her trusted prime minister, Achayya, were reluctant to relinquish their power. They believed that their continued leadership was necessary for the stability and prosperity of the kingdom.

This decision did not sit well with all the factions within the kingdom. Some members of the court and the army felt that it was time for the young king to assume his rightful place on the throne. Tensions rose, and a plot was devised to remove Mangammal and her prime minister from power. The army commander seized them, and they were executed, bringing an abrupt and tragic end to Mangammal's regency.

Despite this sudden and unfortunate conclusion to her rule, Queen Mangammal's legacy endured. Her contributions to the kingdom of Madurai were profound and lasting. The roads she built, the temples she restored, and the policies she implemented continued to benefit the people long after her death. Her life and reign became a source of inspiration for generations to come.

The story of Queen Mangammal is a testament to the power of wisdom, fairness, and compassion. Her reign was marked by significant advancements in infrastructure, culture, and diplomacy. She faced numerous challenges with courage and grace, always prioritizing the well-being of her people. Her legacy lives on in the hearts of those who remember her as a wise and beloved ruler.

One of the most enduring symbols of Mangammal's reign is the highway from Cape Comorin, known as Rani Mangammal Salai. This highway, originally built during her time, facilitated trade and travel, connecting distant parts of the kingdom and beyond. It stands as a testament to her foresight and commitment to improving the lives of her subjects.

Mangammal's contributions to infrastructure extended beyond roads. She recognized the importance of water management in sustaining the agrarian economy of Madurai. She repaired and expanded irrigation channels, ensuring a steady supply of water to the fields. These efforts resulted in increased agricultural productivity, leading to prosperity and stability in the kingdom.

The queen also took a keen interest in architecture. Her "Spring Palace" at TumKum (Thamukkam) was a marvel of design and engineering. This palace, which later became the Gandhi Memorial Museum, showcased her vision and attention to detail. The beautiful gardens, intricate carvings, and serene ambiance of the palace reflected her aesthetic sensibilities and her dedication to creating spaces that brought joy and comfort to her people.

Mangammal's architectural projects were not limited to palaces. She commissioned the construction and renovation of numerous temples, each a masterpiece in its own right. These temples not only served as places of worship but also as centers of community life, where people could gather, celebrate, and seek solace. Her contributions to religious architecture helped preserve the cultural and spiritual heritage of Madurai.

In addition to her architectural and infrastructural achievements, Queen Mangammal was known for her innovative policies that promoted social welfare. She established several choultries, or rest houses, along major travel routes. These choultries provided shelter and food to travelers and pilgrims, ensuring their safety and comfort. This act of kindness and hospitality endeared her to people from all walks of life, reinforcing her image as a compassionate and caring ruler.

Mangammal's governance was characterized by a deep sense of justice. She was known for her fair and impartial judgments, and her court was a place where people could seek redress for their grievances. Her dedication to justice earned her the respect and admiration of her subjects, who saw her as a protector of their rights and well-being.

Her diplomatic skills were further highlighted in her interactions with neighboring kingdoms. Mangammal maintained peaceful relations with other rulers, using diplomacy to resolve conflicts and build alliances. Her ability to navigate the complex political landscape of the time ensured the stability and security of Madurai. Her reign was marked by a period of relative peace and prosperity, allowing her to focus on the development and welfare of her kingdom.

Mangammal's love for her people was evident in every aspect of her rule. She worked tirelessly to improve their lives, whether through infrastructure projects, social welfare initiatives, or fair governance. Her reign was a golden era for Madurai, and her legacy continued to inspire future generations.

As Mangammal's regency progressed, her influence and reputation grew beyond the borders of Madurai. She became a respected figure among the rulers of southern India, known for her wisdom and strength. Her ability to balance power and compassion set her apart as a leader of exceptional caliber.

One of the most challenging periods of her regency was the Siege of Jinji. This prolonged military campaign tested her strategic and diplomatic skills to the utmost. Rajaram, the Maratha prince, had taken refuge in the formidable Jinji fort, and his presence posed a significant threat to the stability of the region. Mangammal understood the importance of neutralizing this threat and joined forces with Zulfiqar Khan, the Mughal general.

The siege lasted for eight long years, marked by numerous battles and strategic maneuvers. Throughout this period, Mangammal displayed remarkable resilience and determination. She coordinated her forces with those of the Mughals, providing crucial support that ultimately led to the capture of the fort. This victory was a testament to her military acumen and her ability to forge effective alliances.

The fall of Jinji not only secured Madurai from external threats but also solidified Mangammal's position as a powerful and capable ruler. Her successful handling of the siege earned her respect from both her allies and adversaries. It was a defining moment in her regency, showcasing her leadership qualities and her unwavering commitment to protecting her kingdom.

Beyond her military and diplomatic achievements, Queen Mangammal's reign was marked by her efforts to foster a sense of unity and cultural pride among her people. She understood that a strong and cohesive society was essential for the prosperity of her kingdom. To this end, she encouraged the celebration of festivals and cultural events that brought people together.

The Unjal festival, introduced by Mangammal, became one of the most popular and cherished celebrations in Madurai. Held in the Meenakshi Temple, this festival featured vibrant processions, music, and dance. It was a time when the entire community came together to honor the goddess Meenakshi Amman and celebrate their shared heritage. The festival not only strengthened the cultural fabric of Madurai but also reinforced the bond between the ruler and her subjects.

Mangammal's support for the arts extended to various forms of cultural expression. She patronized poets, musicians, and artists, creating an environment where creativity could flourish. Her court became a hub of cultural activity, attracting talent from far and wide. This patronage of the arts enriched the cultural landscape of Madurai, leaving a lasting legacy that continued to inspire future generations.

Education was another area where Mangammal made significant contributions. She believed in the power of knowledge and ensured that educational institutions were well-supported. Scholars and students received patronage, and the kingdom became a center of learning. This emphasis on education helped cultivate a well-informed and enlightened populace, contributing to the overall progress of the kingdom.

Mangammal's dedication to improving the lives of her people extended to her innovative approaches to governance. She introduced several policies aimed at enhancing the efficiency and effectiveness of the administration. These reforms streamlined the functioning of the government and ensured that resources were utilized optimally for the benefit of the kingdom.

One of her notable administrative reforms was the establishment of a structured tax system. Mangammal understood that a fair and efficient tax system was crucial for the economic stability of the kingdom. She implemented measures to ensure that taxes were collected fairly and used for public welfare projects. This approach not only increased the kingdom's revenue but also earned her the trust and support of her subjects.

Mangammal also focused on improving the judicial system. She believed that justice should be accessible to all, regardless of their social or economic status. Her court was known for its transparency and fairness, and she personally oversaw many important cases. Her commitment to justice and equity reinforced her reputation as a just and compassionate ruler.

Under Mangammal's rule, Madurai experienced a period of economic growth and prosperity. The improved infrastructure, efficient administration, and supportive policies created an environment conducive to trade and commerce. The kingdom became a thriving hub of economic activity, attracting merchants and traders from distant lands. This economic boom further enhanced the quality of life for the people of Madurai, solidifying Mangammal's legacy as a ruler who truly cared for her subjects.

As Mangammal's grandson, Vijaya Ranga Chokkanatha, approached the age of majority, the question of succession loomed large. Mangammal and her prime minister, Achayya, had governed the kingdom with such effectiveness that many in the court were apprehensive about the transition of power. They feared that the young king might not yet be ready to handle the complexities of rulership.

Despite these concerns, Mangammal understood that it was essential for the continuity of the dynasty and the stability of the kingdom to transition power smoothly. However, her decision to hold on to power for a little longer, believing it to be in the best interest of Madurai, led to growing tensions within the royal court. Different factions emerged, each with their own views on how the kingdom should be governed.

The tension culminated in a dramatic turn of events. The army commander, who believed that it was time for the young king to assume his duties, took decisive action. Mangammal and her prime minister were seized and executed, marking a sudden and tragic end to her regency. This abrupt conclusion was a shock to the kingdom, and the loss of such a wise and beloved leader was deeply felt by her people.

Despite the tragic end, Mangammal's contributions to the kingdom were indelible. Her reign had transformed Madurai, leaving a legacy of development, prosperity, and cultural richness. The roads she built, the temples she restored, and the policies she implemented continued to benefit the kingdom long after her passing. Her memory lived on in the hearts of her people, who remembered her as a queen who ruled with wisdom, fairness, and a deep love for her subjects.

Queen Mangammal's story is one of resilience, wisdom, and compassion. Her life and reign offer valuable lessons in leadership and governance. She demonstrated that a ruler's strength lies not just in their power but in their ability to care for their people and make decisions that benefit the greater good.

Mangammal's contributions to infrastructure, such as the Rani Mangammal Salai, provided a foundation for the kingdom's economic growth. Her efforts in improving irrigation systems ensured that the agrarian economy thrived, leading to prosperity and stability. These physical improvements were matched by her commitment to social welfare, as seen in her establishment of choultries and support for educational institutions.

Her diplomatic skills were equally remarkable. By recognizing Aurangzeb as her suzerain and forging alliances with the Mughal Empire, she secured peace and stability for her kingdom. Her role in the Siege of Jinji showcased her strategic acumen and ability to collaborate with powerful allies to achieve common goals.

Culturally, Mangammal's patronage of the arts and festivals like the Unjal festival enriched the lives of her people. She fostered a sense of unity and pride in their shared heritage, strengthening the social fabric of Madurai. Her support for education ensured that future generations would benefit from knowledge and learning, contributing to the kingdom's long-term progress.

Mangammal's legacy continued to influence the kingdom of Madurai long after her death. The infrastructure projects she initiated remained vital to the kingdom's prosperity, and the cultural institutions she supported continued to thrive. Her contributions to justice and governance set a high standard for future rulers to follow.

One of the most enduring aspects of Mangammal's legacy was her commitment to inclusivity and fairness. She believed that every subject, regardless of their background, deserved to be treated with respect and justice. This philosophy permeated her rule, creating a sense of trust and loyalty among her people. Her dedication to fairness and justice earned her the title of "The Wise Queen," a moniker that reflected her approach to governance.

The memory of Mangammal was preserved through stories and legends passed down through generations. Her life became an inspiration for many, illustrating the impact of compassionate and wise leadership. In schools and homes, children were taught about her achievements and the values she embodied. These stories served as a reminder of the importance of wisdom, justice, and compassion in leadership.

In modern times, efforts to preserve Mangammal's legacy have included the restoration and maintenance of the structures she built. The Gandhi Memorial Museum, housed in her Spring Palace, stands as a tribute to her architectural vision and commitment to public welfare. It serves as a place where people can learn about her life and the rich history of Madurai.

Queen Mangammal's story resonates with people of all ages, but it holds a special place for young readers. Her life is a testament to the idea that true leadership is about serving others and making decisions that benefit the community. For children, her story provides an example of how one person, with wisdom and compassion, can make a significant difference in the world.

Mangammal's reign is a reminder that challenges and obstacles are a part of life, but with determination and the right values, they can be overcome. Her ability to navigate the complexities of governance, handle diplomatic relations, and care for her people illustrates the qualities of a great leader. These lessons are valuable for young readers, who can look up to Mangammal as a role model.

The legacy of Queen Mangammal also highlights the importance of cultural heritage and the need to preserve it. Her efforts in building and restoring temples, supporting the arts, and fostering education ensured that the rich cultural traditions of Madurai were passed down through generations. This emphasis on cultural preservation is a lesson for young readers about the importance of respecting and valuing their heritage.

As young readers learn about Queen Mangammal, they can draw inspiration from her life and achievements. Her story encourages them to pursue their goals with dedication, to act with fairness and compassion, and to contribute positively to their communities. Mangammal's life serves as a beacon of hope and inspiration, reminding them that they, too, can make a difference.

In conclusion, Queen Mangammal's reign was a period of remarkable progress and cultural enrichment for the kingdom of Madurai. Her leadership was defined by her wisdom, fairness, and deep love for her people. Through her infrastructure projects, she laid the foundation for economic growth and stability. Her diplomatic skills ensured peace and security, while her patronage of the arts and education fostered a vibrant cultural landscape.

Mangammal's legacy is a powerful reminder of the impact that a wise and compassionate leader can have on their kingdom. Her story continues to inspire and teach valuable lessons about leadership, justice, and the importance of caring for one's community. As we reflect on her life, we can draw inspiration from her example and strive to embody the values she upheld.

For the children of today, Queen Mangammal's story is a source of inspiration and motivation. It teaches them that with wisdom, courage, and compassion, they can overcome challenges and make a positive difference in the world. Her legacy lives on in the hearts of those who remember her as a wise and beloved ruler, whose contributions to Madurai continue to be celebrated and honored.

Mangammal's life and achievements are a testament to the enduring power of good leadership. Her story will continue to inspire future generations, reminding them of the importance of wisdom, justice, and compassion in building a better world.

CHAPTER SIX

THE JUST KING RAJENDRA CHOLA

In the ancient land of Tamil Nadu, a young prince named Rajendra was born to the mighty king Rajaraja Chola. Rajendra grew up surrounded by tales of valor and wisdom, stories of his father's conquests, and the rich culture of the Chola dynasty. From a young age, Rajendra was curious and eager to learn, often found with his nose buried in scrolls or listening intently to the court's discussions. His father, Rajaraja, was not only a great king but also a loving father who ensured that his son was educated in both the arts of war and peace.

Rajendra's days were filled with lessons from the wisest scholars, training with the bravest warriors, and learning the principles of just rule from his father. Rajaraja often told him, "A true king must be as wise as he is strong, as just as he is brave." These words stayed with Rajendra, shaping his character and guiding his actions.

One day, as the sun cast its golden hue over the palace gardens, Rajaraja called young Rajendra to his side. "Son," he said, "it is time you learn about the responsibilities that come with ruling an empire. You must understand that a king's duty is to serve his people with fairness and compassion."

Eager to prove himself worthy of his lineage, Rajendra listened intently to his father's teachings. Rajaraja narrated tales of great kings from the past, emphasizing the importance of justice and leadership. He recounted how he had expanded the Chola Empire through not just might, but through strategic alliances and benevolent governance.

Rajendra's favorite part of the day was the time he spent with the common people in the markets and villages. Disguised in simple clothes, he would mingle with them, listening to their stories and understanding their needs. These interactions opened his eyes to the challenges faced by his future subjects, and he resolved to be a king who would uplift their lives.

One evening, during a grand feast in the royal court, a messenger arrived with urgent news. A neighboring kingdom was under threat from invaders, and they had sought the help of the Chola Empire. Rajendra watched as his father immediately rallied his generals and planned a defense strategy. This was the first time Rajendra witnessed the responsibilities of kingship in action. He saw how his father's wisdom and decisiveness protected their allies and maintained peace in the region.

Determined to follow in his father's footsteps, Rajendra began his own preparations for leadership. He trained harder, studied longer, and sought advice from his father's trusted advisors. Every lesson was a step towards becoming the just and powerful king his father envisioned.

As Rajendra grew older, his father started involving him more in the affairs of the state. Rajendra attended council meetings, learned about governance, and even made decisions on minor issues. Rajaraja was preparing him for the day he would sit on the throne. One day, Rajaraja took Rajendra to the royal archives, a vast hall filled with scrolls and manuscripts. "These are the chronicles of our ancestors," he said, "their victories, their failures, their wisdom. Study them, for they will teach you what it means to be a true ruler."

Rajendra spent countless hours in the archives, immersing himself in the history of the Chola dynasty. He learned about the great kings who came before him and the principles they upheld. He read about the laws they enacted, the battles they fought, and the temples they built. Each story was a lesson in leadership, justice, and courage.

One scroll, in particular, caught his attention. It detailed the reign of a king who was known for his fairness and compassion. Rajendra was inspired by this king's ability to balance strength with kindness, to lead with a firm hand yet a gentle heart. He decided that this was the kind of king he wanted to be.

As he continued his studies, Rajendra also honed his skills in diplomacy. He learned how to negotiate treaties, forge alliances, and resolve conflicts without resorting to war. His father often said, "The might of a king lies not just in his sword, but in his ability to prevent its use." Rajendra took these words to heart, understanding that true power lay in maintaining peace and justice.

The day finally came when Rajendra would prove his mettle. A rebellion had broken out in a distant province of the empire. Rajaraja, confident in his son's abilities, appointed Rajendra to lead the campaign to quell the uprising. It was Rajendra's first significant test as a leader, and he was determined to succeed.

Rajendra assembled a formidable army and marched towards the rebellious province. Along the way, he ensured that his soldiers were well-fed and cared for, knowing that a content army was a loyal and effective one. He also sent emissaries to the province, offering a peaceful resolution to the conflict. Rajendra believed that diplomacy should always be the first course of action.

However, the rebels were unyielding, and a battle became inevitable. Rajendra led his troops with courage and strategic brilliance, just as he had been taught. He positioned his forces wisely, utilizing the terrain to their advantage, and launched a surprise attack that caught the rebels off guard. The battle was fierce, but Rajendra's leadership and tactical acumen prevailed. The rebellion was swiftly crushed, and peace was restored to the province.

After the battle, Rajendra showed mercy to the captured rebels, offering them a chance to pledge their loyalty to the Chola Empire. Many accepted his offer, grateful for his compassion. Rajendra's actions earned him the respect and admiration of his soldiers and subjects alike. He returned to the capital victorious, his reputation as a just and capable leader firmly established.

Rajendra's success in quelling the rebellion marked the beginning of his illustrious career as a military commander and statesman. His father, Rajaraja, was immensely proud of him. "You have proven yourself to be a true Chola," he said, "one who leads with wisdom and justice." Rajendra knew that this was only the beginning, and he was eager to take on greater responsibilities.

Under Rajaraja's guidance, Rajendra embarked on a series of campaigns to expand the Chola Empire. These were not merely wars of conquest, but missions to spread the prosperity and stability of their kingdom to neighboring lands. Rajendra's sense of justice guided his actions, and he ensured that the people of the conquered territories were treated with respect and fairness.

One of Rajendra's most notable achievements was his naval expedition to the distant lands of Srivijaya, a powerful maritime empire. Rajendra recognized the importance of controlling the sea routes for trade and security. He assembled a grand fleet, the likes of which had never been seen before, and set sail on a daring adventure across the ocean.

The voyage was arduous, with treacherous waters and unpredictable weather. But Rajendra's determination and leadership kept the morale of his sailors high. He treated them as equals, sharing in their hardships and celebrating their victories. This bond between the king and his men was the key to their success.

When they finally reached Srivijaya, Rajendra demonstrated his strategic brilliance once more. He negotiated with the local rulers, offering them favorable terms for joining the Chola Empire. Many agreed, recognizing the benefits of being part of such a prosperous and just realm. For those who resisted, Rajendra's navy displayed its might, securing a swift and decisive victory.

The conquest of Srivijaya was a monumental achievement for the Chola Empire. Rajendra's success in this campaign not only expanded the empire's territory but also established its dominance over the crucial maritime trade routes. This brought immense wealth and prosperity to the Chola kingdom, further solidifying Rajendra's reputation as a great leader.

Upon his return, Rajendra was welcomed with grand celebrations. The people hailed him as a hero, and his father embraced him with pride. Rajaraja declared, "Rajendra, you have surpassed all expectations. You have brought glory to our dynasty and prosperity to our people." Rajendra humbly accepted the accolades, knowing that his journey was far from over.

Rajendra's rule was marked by a deep commitment to justice and fairness. He believed that a king's true strength lay in his ability to ensure the well-being of his subjects. He implemented numerous reforms to improve the lives of the common people. He reduced taxes, built infrastructure, and promoted education. Under his rule, the

Chola Empire flourished, becoming a beacon of culture and prosperity.

One of Rajendra's most beloved policies was his open court sessions. Every week, he would hold an audience where anyone, regardless of their status, could come and present their grievances. Rajendra listened to each case with patience and wisdom, delivering fair judgments that earned him the love and respect of his people.

His reputation as a just king spread far and wide, attracting scholars, artists, and merchants to his court. The Chola Empire became a melting pot of ideas and cultures, enriching its society and fostering a golden age of art and learning. Rajendra's vision of a just and prosperous kingdom was coming to fruition, and his people thrived under his benevolent rule.

Rajendra's sense of justice was not limited to his own empire. He believed in fostering good relations with neighboring kingdoms and sought to create a network of alliances based on mutual respect and cooperation. He often hosted diplomatic missions from other lands, treating the envoys with great honor and hospitality. These interactions helped to strengthen ties and promote peace in the region.

One such mission brought a delegation from a distant kingdom facing a severe drought. The people were suffering, and their king sought Rajendra's assistance. Moved by their plight, Rajendra immediately dispatched resources, including food, water, and skilled engineers to help build irrigation systems. His swift and compassionate response not only alleviated the suffering of the people but also cemented a lasting friendship between the two kingdoms.

Stories of Rajendra's wisdom and fairness spread throughout the land, reaching even the most remote villages. One tale that became particularly popular was about a dispute between two farmers over a piece of land. Unable to resolve the matter themselves, they brought their case before Rajendra. After listening to both sides, Rajendra devised a clever solution: he divided the land equally but gave the farmers the option to work it together and share the produce. The farmers, realizing the benefits of cooperation, agreed, and their combined efforts yielded a bountiful harvest.

Rajendra's reign was filled with such stories of justice and wisdom. His ability to resolve conflicts with fairness and ingenuity made him a beloved figure among his people. He became known not just as a great warrior and conqueror, but as a king who truly cared for the well-being of his subjects.

As the years passed, Rajendra continued to build on his father's legacy, leading the Chola Empire to new heights of glory and prosperity. He invested heavily in infrastructure, constructing grand temples, intricate water management systems, and extensive road networks that connected the vast empire. These projects not only showcased the architectural prowess of the Chola dynasty but also improved the quality of life for the people.

One of Rajendra's most ambitious projects was the construction of the Gangaikonda Cholapuram, a magnificent city that served as the new capital of the empire. The city was designed to be a symbol of Chola power and cultural achievement. At its heart stood the Brihadisvara Temple, a towering structure adorned with intricate carvings and sculptures that depicted the rich heritage and spiritual devotion of the Chola people.

Gangaikonda Cholapuram became a thriving center of commerce, culture, and learning. Scholars from across the world flocked to the city, drawn by the promise of patronage and intellectual exchange. Rajendra encouraged these scholars, providing them with resources and opportunities to advance their studies. The city's libraries and universities became renowned centers of knowledge, contributing to the empire's reputation as a beacon of wisdom and enlightenment.

Rajendra's rule was also marked by a deep sense of responsibility towards the environment. He understood the importance of sustainable development and implemented policies to protect the natural resources of his kingdom. Forests were preserved, rivers were kept clean, and wildlife was protected. Rajendra's vision of harmony between man and nature ensured that the Chola Empire thrived without depleting its natural wealth.

Rajendra's dedication to justice and prosperity extended to all corners of his empire. He established a network of local administrators, each carefully chosen for their integrity and competence. These officials were responsible for maintaining law and order, collecting taxes, and ensuring that the needs of the people were met. Rajendra personally oversaw their training, emphasizing the importance of fairness and compassion in governance.

One day, during a routine inspection of a distant province, Rajendra encountered a group of villagers gathered around a young boy who had lost his parents in a tragic accident. The villagers were concerned about the boy's future, unsure of how to care for him. Rajendra listened to their worries and decided to take the boy under his wing. He arranged for the boy's education and upbringing, ensuring that he had every opportunity to succeed. This act of kindness further endeared Rajendra to his people, reinforcing his image as a compassionate and just ruler.

Rajendra's policies also focused on empowering women and ensuring their participation in the empire's development. He encouraged education for girls, provided opportunities for women to engage in trade and crafts, and supported their involvement in community decision-making. Under his rule, women enjoyed greater freedom and respect, contributing significantly to the prosperity and cultural rich-ness of the Chola Empire.

The king's dedication to justice and equality fostered a sense of unity and pride among his subjects. People from diverse backgrounds and communities felt a deep connection to the Chola dynasty, and their collective efforts propelled the empire to unprecedented heights. Rajendra's vision of an inclusive and prosperous society became a reality, leaving an indelible mark on the history of the Chola Empire.

Rajendra's leadership and vision transformed the Chola Empire into a shining example of justice, prosperity, and cultural achievement. His reign was a golden age, marked by significant advancements in art, science, and architecture. The empire's prosperity allowed for the flourishing of various art forms, including music, dance, and litera-ture. Rajendra himself was a patron of the arts, often inviting poets and artists to his court to showcase their talents.

One evening, during a grand cultural festival in the capital, Ra-jendra was approached by a young poet who had written a beautiful poem about the harmony between man and nature. The poet recited his work with such passion that it moved everyone present, including Rajendra. The king was deeply impressed by the poet's talent and offered him a place at the royal court. This gesture not only highlighted Rajendra's appreciation for the arts but also inspired others to pursue their creative passions.

Rajendra's commitment to justice was also evident in his interac-tions with his court and advisors. He valued their counsel and encour-aged open discussions, ensuring that every voice was heard. His court was a place where ideas flowed freely, and decisions were made based on collective wisdom. This inclusive approach to governance fostered a sense of loyalty and respect among his advisors, who were dedicated to serving the empire with integrity and diligence.

The king's fair and just rule extended to the administration of justice. Rajendra established a system of courts where disputes could be resolved peacefully and fairly. He appointed wise and impartial judges who upheld the law without fear or favor. This judicial system ensured that everyone, regardless of their status, had access to justice. Rajendra's unwavering commitment to fairness and equality made the Chola Empire a model of good governance.

Rajendra's reputation as a just and wise ruler spread far and wide, attracting visitors from distant lands who came to witness the grandeur of the Chola Empire. Among these visitors were scholars, traders, and diplomats, each bringing their own unique perspectives and experiences. Rajendra welcomed them all with open arms, eager to learn from their knowledge and share the wealth of his own empire.

One such visitor was a renowned philosopher from a distant land who had heard tales of Rajendra's wisdom and justice. The philosopher requested an audience with the king to discuss matters of governance and philosophy. Rajendra, always eager to engage in meaningful dialogue, welcomed the philosopher to his court. Their discussions covered a wide range of topics, from the principles of justice to the responsibilities of a ruler. Rajendra's insightful questions and thoughtful responses impressed the philosopher, who marveled at the king's intellect and compassion.

Inspired by their conversations, Rajendra implemented new policies that further strengthened the governance of his empire. He introduced reforms to improve transparency and accountability in administration, ensuring that officials acted in the best interests of the people. These reforms not only enhanced the efficiency of the government but also increased public trust in the king's leadership.

Rajendra's interactions with the philosopher also influenced his personal beliefs and values. He became more reflective, often contemplating the deeper meaning of justice and the true purpose of leadership. These reflections guided his decisions and actions, reinforcing his commitment to serving his people with fairness and compassion.

Throughout his reign, Rajendra faced numerous challenges, but his unwavering commitment to justice and his steadfast leadership always saw him through. One of the most significant challenges came when a coalition of rival kingdoms threatened to invade the Chola Empire. These kingdoms, envious of the Chola's prosperity and power, sought to destabilize Rajendra's rule.

Rajendra, ever the strategic thinker, prepared for the impending conflict with meticulous planning. He strengthened the empire's defenses, trained his army rigorously, and forged alliances with neighboring friendly kingdoms. He also sent envoys to negotiate with the rival kingdoms, offering terms of peace and cooperation. Rajendra believed that diplomacy should always be the first course of action, but he was also prepared to defend his empire with all his might.

Despite his efforts, the rival kingdoms launched their invasion. The battles that ensued were fierce, but Rajendra's leadership and the loyalty of his people and soldiers turned the tide in favor of the Chola Empire. Rajendra led his troops with unparalleled bravery, inspiring them with his courage and determination. His strategic brilliance and unwavering resolve ensured that the Chola Empire emerged victorious.

After the war, Rajendra focused on rebuilding and healing the wounds of conflict. He extended a hand of friendship to the defeated kingdoms, offering them fair terms and opportunities to rebuild their own lands. This act of magnanimity not only secured lasting peace but also strengthened the bonds between the Chola Empire and its neighbors.

Rajendra's ability to balance strength with compassion, to lead with justice and fairness, solidified his legacy as one of the greatest kings in the history of the Chola dynasty. His reign became a benchmark for future generations, a testament to the power of just and enlightened leadership.

Rajendra's contributions to the Chola Empire extended beyond his military and administrative achievements. He was a visionary leader who understood the importance of education and knowledge. He established numerous schools and universities, ensuring that the children of the empire had access to quality education. Rajendra believed that an educated populace was the foundation of a prosperous and just society.

Under his patronage, the arts and sciences flourished. The royal court became a hub of intellectual activity, attracting scholars, poets, artists, and scientists from all over the world. Rajendra encouraged the exchange of ideas and knowledge, fostering an environment of creativity and innovation. This cultural renaissance enriched the empire and left a lasting legacy that continued to inspire future generations.

One of Rajendra's most notable initiatives was the establishment of a grand library in the capital. This library housed an extensive collection of manuscripts and texts on various subjects, including literature, philosophy, science, and history. Scholars from far and wide came to study and share their knowledge, contributing to the advancement of learning in the Chola Empire. Rajendra's investment in education and culture ensured that his people were not only prosperous but also enlightened.

Rajendra's reign was also marked by significant advancements in technology and engineering. His support for innovative projects led to the development of sophisticated irrigation systems, architectural marvels, and efficient administrative practices. These advancements

improved the quality of life for the people and showcased the ingenuity and resourcefulness of the Chola dynasty.

As Rajendra grew older, he began to reflect on his legacy and the
future of the Chola Empire. He spent more time mentoring the next
generation of leaders, passing on his wisdom and experience. Rajendra's vision for a just and prosperous empire continued to guide his
actions, ensuring that his legacy would endure long after his reign.

Rajendra's later years were filled with moments of reflection and
planning for the future. He understood the importance of a smooth
transition of power and began to prepare his son, Rajadhiraja Chola,
to take over the responsibilities of the throne. Rajendra's teachings
focused on the same principles of justice, compassion, and wisdom
that had guided his own rule.

Rajadhiraja was an eager student, absorbing the lessons from his
father with great enthusiasm. Rajendra often took him on tours of the
empire, showing him the various regions and explaining the intricacies
of governance. He introduced him to the key advisors and officials,
ensuring that Rajadhiraja built strong relationships and understood
the workings of the empire.

During these tours, Rajendra would also take the time to visit
the common people, listening to their concerns and celebrating their
successes. He wanted Rajadhiraja to understand that the true strength
of the Chola Empire lay in its people. "A king's duty is to serve his
subjects," he would often say, "for their well-being is the measure of
his success."

One day, while visiting a remote village, Rajendra and Rajadhiraja
came across an elderly woman who was renowned for her wisdom. She
shared with them stories of the village's history and the challenges they
had overcome. Rajendra listened intently, appreciating the rich tapes-
try of experiences that shaped the lives of his people. He encouraged

Rajadhiraja to do the same, to always seek the wisdom of others and to lead with empathy and understanding.

Rajendra's dedication to preparing his son for leadership ensured that the Chola Empire would continue to thrive under Rajadhiraja's rule. The values of justice, compassion, and wisdom that had defined Rajendra's reign would live on, guiding the empire into a new era of prosperity and greatness.

As Rajendra's reign drew to a close, the entire Chola Empire came together to celebrate his legacy. Grand festivities were held in his honor, with people from all walks of life participating in the celebrations. The streets of the capital were adorned with vibrant decorations, and the air was filled with the sound of music and laughter. It was a fitting tribute to a king who had dedicated his life to the service of his people.

Rajendra took this opportunity to address his subjects one last time. Standing before a sea of faces, he spoke with humility and gratitude. "My beloved people," he began, "it has been my greatest honor to serve as your king. Together, we have built an empire that stands as a beacon of justice, prosperity, and wisdom. I am confident that under the leadership of my son, Rajadhiraja, this legacy will continue to flourish."

The crowd erupted in applause, their cheers echoing across the city. Rajendra's words were a testament to his deep love and respect for his people. As he looked out at the sea of smiling faces, he felt a profound sense of fulfillment. His life's work had been dedicated to creating a just and prosperous kingdom, and seeing the joy and pride of his subjects was the greatest reward he could have hoped for.

In the twilight of his reign, Rajendra continued to serve as a guiding light for the Chola Empire. His wisdom and counsel were sought by many, and his legacy of justice and compassion inspired future generations. Rajendra Chola, the just and wise king, had left an indelible mark on history, ensuring that the Chola Empire would be remembered as one of the greatest civilizations of its time.

CHAPTER SEVEN

THE CHARITABLE QUEEN SEMBIYAN MAHADEVI

Once upon a time, in the grand Chola Empire of southern India, there lived a queen named Sembiyan Mahadevi. She was not only known for her royal status but also for her kind heart and generous spirit. Sembiyan Mahadevi was married to Gandaraditya Chola, the emperor of the Chola Empire, and together, they ruled with wisdom and compassion.

Queen Sembiyan Mahadevi had a deep love for art, culture, and spirituality. She believed that temples were not just places of worship but also centers of learning and community gatherings. Her reign as queen consort from 949 CE to 957 CE was marked by her tireless efforts in promoting these values. She oversaw the construction of numerous temples across the kingdom, each more magnificent than the last. These temples were not just architectural marvels; they were also filled with beautiful sculptures and carvings that depicted stories from ancient scriptures.

One of the most famous temples she built was in the town of Kutralam. This temple, dedicated to Lord Shiva, became a beacon of hope and spirituality for the people. The temple's towering gopuram, or entrance tower, was adorned with intricate carvings of gods, goddesses, and mythical creatures. The temple courtyard was always bustling with activity, as devotees gathered to offer their prayers and seek blessings.

Queen Sembiyan Mahadevi's contributions to the Chola Empire were not limited to temple building alone. She was also known for her generous endowments to these sacred places. One of her most notable acts of charity was the endowment of a lamp that would remain perpetually lit in front of the deity in the temple. This lamp symbolized the eternal light of knowledge and faith, a guiding beacon for all who came to the temple seeking solace and wisdom.

After the untimely death of her husband, Gandaraditya Chola, Sembiyan Mahadevi's life took a sorrowful turn. She lost her titles as queen and empress and became known as the Queen Dowager of Thanjavur. In mourning for her beloved husband, she chose to wear only white, the color of grief, for the rest of her life. Despite her personal sorrow, her dedication to her people and her faith never wavered.

As the mother of Uttama Chola, she played a crucial role in his upbringing and education. She ensured that he was not only well-versed in the arts of governance and warfare but also imbued with a deep sense of compassion and justice. Her influence on Uttama Chola was profound, and he grew up to be a wise and just ruler, much like his mother.

Sembiyan Mahadevi was not only a devoted mother but also a beloved figure among her subjects. The people of the Chola Empire revered her for her kindness and generosity. She often traveled throughout the kingdom, visiting villages and towns to understand the needs of her people. Her presence was always met with joy and gratitude, as she brought hope and relief to many.

One of her most cherished contributions was the establishment of schools and learning centers within the temple complexes. She believed that education was the key to empowering her people and ensuring the prosperity of the kingdom. These schools provided free education to children from all backgrounds, teaching them not only religious texts but also subjects like mathematics, science, and the arts. Under her patronage, the Chola Empire became a center of learning and culture, attracting scholars and artists from far and wide.

Queen Sembiyan Mahadevi also supported the creation of exquisite bronze sculptures, which became famous throughout the land. These bronzes, often depicting deities in intricate poses, were not just works of art but also expressions of devotion and spirituality. One such bronze, a depiction of the goddess Uma Paramesvari, still worshipped today, is a testament to her legacy as a patron of the arts.

In addition to her support for art and education, Queen Sembiyan Mahadevi was deeply committed to the welfare of her people. She initiated numerous charitable projects to help those in need. During times of drought or famine, she organized relief efforts to ensure that no one went hungry. Her compassion extended to all living beings, and she often provided funds for the care of animals, especially in the temples where they were revered as sacred.

Sembiyan Mahadevi's devotion to Lord Shiva was legendary. She believed that serving the deity was equivalent to serving her people. Her personal piety inspired many, and she was often seen participating in religious ceremonies and rituals. Her favorite temple was the Chidambaram Nataraja Temple, dedicated to Lord Shiva in his form as the cosmic dancer, Nataraja. It was said that she made significant contributions to this temple, including the endowment of lamps and the organization of grand festivals in honor of the deity.

Despite the loss of her royal titles, Sembiyan Mahadevi continued to be a powerful and influential figure in the Chola Empire. Her wisdom and guidance were sought by many, including her son, Uttama Chola. She remained a pillar of strength and a source of inspiration, embodying the virtues of compassion, humility, and devotion.

As the years passed, Queen Sembiyan Mahadevi's legacy only grew stronger. Her contributions to the arts, culture, and spirituality left an indelible mark on the Chola Empire. The temples she built and endowed became centers of learning and culture, attracting pilgrims, scholars, and artists from all over the region. These temples were not only places of worship but also served as hubs for community gatherings, festivals, and cultural events.

One of the most significant temples she built was the Tiru-Ara-neri-Alvar temple. This temple, with its stunning architecture and intricate sculptures, became a symbol of the Chola Empire's artistic and spiritual achievements. The temple was adorned with beautiful bronzes and jewelry, many of which were gifted by Sembiyan Mahadevi herself. These gifts included a bronze idol of the goddess Uma Paramesvari, which is still worshipped in the temple today.

Her dedication to preserving and promoting the arts extended beyond temple building. She supported the creation of bronze sculptures that depicted various deities in graceful and dynamic poses. These bronzes, known for their intricate details and lifelike expressions, became iconic representations of the Chola artistic tradition. The bronzes often depicted the gods in poses that conveyed their divine attributes and powers, capturing the imagination of worshippers and art enthusiasts alike.

Queen Sembiyan Mahadevi's influence also extended to the rituals and ceremonies held in the temples. She was known for organizing grand festivals that brought the entire community together in celebration. One such festival was the śribali ceremony, held every month at the UmaMahesvarasvamin temple in Konerirajapuram. This ceremony, which took place on the day of jyeshta, the natal star of the queen, involved elaborate rituals and offerings. The queen provided generous endowments to ensure that the ceremony was conducted with grandeur and reverence.

Her devotion to Lord Shiva was reflected in the meticulous care she took in maintaining the temples and their rituals. She ensured that the temples were always well-stocked with supplies for the daily worship and that the priests were well-compensated for their services. Her attention to detail and her unwavering faith made her a beloved figure among the temple priests and devotees.

Sembiyan Mahadevi's life was a testament to the power of faith and compassion. Even in her later years, when she had withdrawn from the royal court, she continued to be actively involved in charitable and religious activities. Her residence in Thanjavur became a place of refuge and support for many, as she opened her doors to those in need and provided them with food, shelter, and medical care.

Queen Sembiyan Mahadevi's charitable works were not limited to the grand gestures of temple building and endowments. She was known for her personal acts of kindness and generosity. She often visited villages and towns, offering support to the sick and the poor. Her presence brought comfort and hope to many, and she was affectionately referred to as the "Mother of the People."

Her compassion extended to all creatures, great and small. She believed in the sanctity of all life and often funded shelters for animals, ensuring that they were cared for and protected. Her love for animals was well-known, and she was often seen feeding the birds and animals that lived in the temple grounds. This deep sense of empathy and kindness endeared her to everyone who knew her.

One of the most touching stories about Sembiyan Mahadevi is how she once helped a group of orphaned children. She provided them with food, clothing, and education, ensuring that they had a bright future ahead. Her actions inspired others in the community to come forward and help those in need, creating a ripple effect of kindness and generosity throughout the kingdom.

Queen Sembiyan Mahadevi's life was a shining example of how one person's compassion and dedication could transform an entire community. Her legacy of love and service continued to inspire generations long after her time.

Sembiyan Mahadevi's influence on the Chola Empire was evident in the way the kingdom flourished during and after her time. The temples she built were not only places of worship but also centers of economic activity. Artisans, craftsmen, and traders thrived around these temples, contributing to the prosperity of the region. The temple towns became bustling hubs of commerce, where goods and ideas were exchanged, and the cultural fabric of the empire was enriched.

The queen's patronage of the arts also had a profound impact on the Chola society. The exquisite bronzes and sculptures that were created under her sponsorship became masterpieces of Chola art. These artworks were not only beautiful but also served as important religious symbols, inspiring devotion and reverence among the worshippers. The bronzes, with their intricate details and lifelike forms, captured the grace and power of the deities, bringing them to life for the devotees.

Queen Sembiyan Mahadevi's legacy was also preserved in the form of inscriptions and records. These inscriptions, found in the temples she built, detailed her contributions and the endowments she made. They served as a testament to her devotion and generosity, ensuring that her memory would be honored for generations to come. Through these inscriptions, the stories of her kindness and her unwavering faith were passed down, inspiring others to follow in her footsteps.

One of the most enduring symbols of Queen Sembiyan Mahadevi's legacy was the town of Sembiyan Mahadevi, named in her honor. This town, centered around a grand Shiva temple, became a place of pilgrimage and reverence. Every year, on the queen's birthday, special celebrations were held in the temple to honor her memory. These celebrations included processions, music, dance, and offerings, and people from all over the kingdom would come to participate.

A particularly cherished part of these celebrations was the display of a bronze portrait of Sembiyan Mahadevi. This highly stylized image depicted her in a pose reminiscent of the goddess Parvati, symbolizing her divine qualities and her deep spiritual connection. The bronze, with its intricate details and elegant form, was carried in processions, allowing the people to pay their respects and seek her blessings.

The queen's influence was also evident in the daily lives of the people. Her emphasis on education and learning had a lasting impact on the kingdom. The schools and learning centers she established continued to thrive, producing scholars, poets, and artists who contributed to the rich cultural heritage of the Chola Empire. Her commitment to the welfare of her people ensured that the kingdom remained prosperous and harmonious, with a strong sense of community and shared values.

The story of Queen Sembiyan Mahadevi's life was one of resilience and unwavering faith. Despite the challenges she faced, including the loss of her husband and her royal titles, she remained dedicated to her people and her beliefs. Her strength and determination were a source of inspiration for many, and her legacy continued to shape the Chola Empire long after her time.

Sembiyan Mahadevi's devotion to Lord Shiva was a central aspect of her life. She believed that through her service to the deity, she was serving her people. This belief was reflected in everything she did, from the temples she built to the charitable acts she performed. Her life was a testament to the power of faith and the impact that one person's compassion and dedication can have on an entire community.

As the years went by, the Chola Empire continued to thrive, and the temples built by Sembiyan Mahadevi remained important centers of worship and culture. The bronzes and sculptures she sponsored continued to be admired for their beauty and craftsmanship, and the inscriptions detailing her contributions ensured that her memory was preserved.

Her story was passed down through generations, inspiring countless others to follow her example of kindness, generosity, and devotion. Queen Sembiyan Mahadevi's life was a shining beacon of hope and compassion, a legacy that would be remembered and cherished for centuries.

The influence of Queen Sembiyan Mahadevi extended beyond the borders of the Chola Empire. Her dedication to temple building and the arts attracted the attention of scholars and artists from other regions. They came to learn from the Chola artisans, study the inscriptions, and witness the grand temples she had built. Her contributions helped to spread the fame of the Chola Empire far and wide, making it a center of culture and learning.

In recognition of her contributions, many temples across South India held special ceremonies in her honor. These ceremonies often included the recitation of prayers, the lighting of lamps, and the offering of flowers and sweets to the deities. The people would gather in large numbers to participate in these events, celebrating the legacy of a queen who had given so much to her kingdom.

The impact of Sembiyan Mahadevi's work on the arts was particularly significant. The bronzes and sculptures created under her patronage became the standard of excellence for future generations of artists. The techniques and styles developed during her time influenced the art of the region for centuries, and many of the artworks from this period are considered masterpieces of Indian art.

Even today, the name of Sembiyan Mahadevi is synonymous with compassion, devotion, and artistic excellence. Her legacy lives on in the temples she built, the art she inspired, and the countless lives she touched with her kindness and generosity. Her story continues to inspire and remind us of the power of faith and the importance of serving others.

Queen Sembiyan Mahadevi's contributions were not just limited to grand temples and sculptures; she also made significant efforts to improve the daily lives of her people. She introduced various initiatives to enhance agricultural productivity, ensuring that her kingdom remained self-sufficient and prosperous. Her policies encouraged the use of advanced farming techniques, which led to increased crop yields and better food security for the people.

The queen's focus on education and healthcare was also instrumental in improving the quality of life in the Chola Empire. She supported the establishment of hospitals and clinics, where people could receive medical care free of charge. These healthcare facilities were often located near temples, reflecting her belief in the connection between physical well-being and spiritual health.

Her emphasis on education extended to women as well. Sembiyan Mahadevi believed that empowering women through education was crucial for the overall progress of society. She encouraged the establishment of schools for girls, where they could learn to read, write, and acquire various skills. This initiative not only improved the status of women in the kingdom but also contributed to the intellectual and cultural growth of the Chola Empire.

Queen Sembiyan Mahadevi's forward-thinking policies and her dedication to the welfare of her people created a strong and resilient society. Her reign was marked by peace, prosperity, and cultural flourishing, and her legacy continued to shape the Chola Empire for generations.

The lasting impact of Queen Sembiyan Mahadevi's reign can be seen in the enduring prosperity of the Chola Empire. Her contributions to art, culture, and society created a solid foundation for future generations to build upon. The temples she built remained vibrant centers of worship and community life, and the schools and hospitals she established continued to serve the people.

One of the most remarkable aspects of her legacy was the way she balanced her royal duties with her personal faith and compassion. Despite the demands of her position, she always found time to care for her people and ensure their well-being. Her life was a testament to the idea that true leadership involves not just power and authority but also empathy and service.

Queen Sembiyan Mahadevi's story was passed down through generations, becoming a source of inspiration for many. Parents would tell their children about the kind and wise queen who built temples, supported artists, and cared for the poor. Her example encouraged others to act with kindness and generosity, creating a culture of compassion and service in the Chola Empire.

Even today, her legacy is celebrated in various ways. Festivals and ceremonies are held in her honor, and her contributions to art and culture are studied and admired. The story of Queen Sembiyan Mahadevi reminds us that one person's dedication and compassion can make a profound difference in the world.

As we reflect on the life and legacy of Queen Sembiyan Mahadevi, it is clear that her contributions went far beyond the physical structures she built. Her true legacy lay in the values she embodied and instilled in her people—values of compassion, generosity, and a deep commitment to the welfare of others. Her reign was a shining example of how a leader's actions can positively impact the lives of countless individuals and shape the course of history.

Sembiyan Mahadevi's story is a reminder of the importance of preserving our cultural heritage and honoring those who came before us. The temples she built, the bronzes she commissioned, and the schools she founded are all tangible reminders of her vision and dedication. These structures serve as a link between the past and the present, allowing us to connect with the rich history and culture of the Chola Empire.

The queen's legacy also highlights the enduring power of faith and devotion. Her unwavering commitment to Lord Shiva and her belief in the power of spirituality to transform lives inspired many. Her life story continues to inspire devotion and reverence among those who learn about her, reminding us of the timeless values of faith, service, and compassion.

Queen Sembiyan Mahadevi's life and legacy are a testament to the idea that true greatness lies not in wealth or power, but in the love and care we show to others. Her story is a beacon of hope and inspiration, guiding us to lead lives of purpose and kindness.

In the annals of history, Queen Sembiyan Mahadevi stands out as a remarkable figure whose contributions transcended her time. Her story is not just one of a queen who ruled with wisdom and grace, but of a compassionate soul who dedicated her life to the service of others.

Her impact on the Chola Empire and its people was profound, and her legacy continues to be felt even today.

The temples she built are still places of worship and cultural significance, drawing visitors from all over the world. The bronzes she commissioned are admired for their artistic brilliance and serve as a testament to the high standards of Chola craftsmanship. The educational and healthcare institutions she founded laid the groundwork for a society that valued knowledge and well-being.

Queen Sembiyan Mahadevi's life is a reminder that each of us has the power to make a difference. Her story encourages us to look beyond our own lives and consider how we can contribute to the greater good. Whether through acts of kindness, support for the arts, or efforts to improve our communities, we can all follow her example and leave a lasting legacy of compassion and service.

As we celebrate the life of Queen Sembiyan Mahadevi, let us be inspired by her dedication and generosity. Let her story remind us of the importance of faith, the power of compassion, and the enduring impact of a life lived in service to others.

Chapter Eight

Legendary King Pandyan Nedunchezhiyan

In the ancient land of Tamil Nadu, where the rivers flowed like silver threads and the mountains stood tall like silent guardians, there was a young prince named Nedunchezhiyan. He belonged to the mighty Pandya dynasty, known for their wisdom, courage, and love for their people. The Pandya kings were not just rulers; they were the protectors of their land, patrons of the arts, and champions of justice.

Nedunchezhiyan was only fifteen years old when he ascended the throne, after the untimely demise of his parents. Despite his young age, he possessed a sharp mind and a heart full of bravery. His eyes sparkled with determination, and his every step echoed with the promise of greatness. The people of his kingdom looked up to him with hope, believing in his potential to be a strong and just ruler.

One fateful day, news arrived that the neighboring kingdoms of Chera and Chola were planning to invade the Pandya territory. These kingdoms, rich in culture and history, had united against the Pandyas, seeing the young king as an easy target. But little did they know, King Nedunchezhiyan was not one to be underestimated.

Upon hearing the news of the impending invasion, King Nedunchezhiyan gathered his council of advisors. Among them was the wise and loyal Chief Bard Maangudi Maruthanaar, known for his poetic praises and strategic mind. The young king listened intently as his advisors spoke of the threats and challenges that lay ahead. He knew that the fate of his kingdom rested on his shoulders, and he was determined to protect his people at all costs.

King Nedunchezhiyan decided to take action. He summoned his army, a formidable force of brave warriors and skilled archers. The young king himself led the troops, riding at the front on his majestic elephant. His presence inspired courage and confidence among his soldiers, and they marched forward with unwavering determination.

The battlefield was set at Talaiyalanganam, a strategic location near Tiruvarur. The opposing armies of the Cheras and Cholas were vast and powerful, but King Nedunchezhiyan's strategic mind and courageous spirit gave his forces a unique advantage. As the two armies clashed, the young king fought valiantly, leading his men with skill and bravery.

Amidst the chaos of battle, King Nedunchezhiyan's sharp eyes caught sight of the Chera king, Mandaranjeral Irumporai. With a swift and calculated move, Nedunchezhiyan charged forward, his spear gleaming under the sun. He penetrated the enemy's ranks like a ship cutting through the waves, his warriors following close behind.

The Chera king was captured, and the morale of the enemy forces began to crumble. The sight of their king in chains struck fear into their hearts, and the once mighty armies of Chera and Chola began to retreat. Victory was within reach, and King Nedunchezhiyan did not relent. He pursued the fleeing enemies deep into Chola territory, ensuring that they would not dare to challenge the Pandya kingdom again.

News of the triumphant victory spread like wildfire across the land. The people of Pandya celebrated their young king's bravery and strategic prowess. Songs of his valor were sung in every village and town, and the kingdom rejoiced in the newfound peace and security.

With the threat of invasion quelled, King Nedunchezhiyan turned his attention to strengthening his kingdom. He knew that true strength lay not just in military might but in the prosperity and happiness of his people. He initiated various projects to improve the infrastructure of his kingdom, building roads, irrigation systems, and trade routes that connected different regions.

The capital city of Madurai flourished under his reign, becoming a hub of culture, trade, and learning. Scholars, poets, and artists from all over the Tamil country flocked to the city, drawn by the king's patronage and the promise of a vibrant intellectual community. The famous Sangam assemblies, where poets and scholars gathered to share their works, were held regularly, enriching the cultural heritage of the Pandya kingdom.

King Nedunchezhiyan also focused on ensuring justice and fairness in his realm. He established courts and appointed wise judges to oversee the administration of justice. The young king was known for his compassion and his ability to listen to the grievances of his people. He would often disguise himself and walk among his subjects, learning about their lives and addressing their concerns directly.

One day, while walking through a bustling marketplace in disguise, King Nedunchezhiyan overheard a conversation that piqued his interest. A group of traders were discussing the wealth and prosperity of a distant land known for its precious pearls and exotic spices. The young king realized that expanding trade could bring great benefits to his kingdom.

Determined to establish strong trade relations, King Nedunchezhiyan set out on a diplomatic mission. He traveled to the chief trading port of Korkai, a bustling harbor where merchants from distant lands gathered. The king met with traders from China, Rome, and Athens, negotiating deals and forging alliances that would bring wealth and prosperity to the Pandya kingdom.

The chief commodity traded was the sea conch pearls, highly valued for their beauty and rarity. Along with pearls, the kingdom traded cotton, ivory, pepper, and sandalwood, receiving gold and gems in return. These trade relations not only enriched the kingdom but also strengthened its position as a major player in the global economy of the time.

As the Pandya kingdom grew in wealth and influence, King Nedunchezhiyan continued to face challenges. The neighboring kingdoms, although defeated in battle, still harbored ambitions of power and dominance. The young king knew that maintaining peace required constant vigilance and strategic planning.

To ensure the security of his kingdom, King Nedunchezhiyan established a network of alliances with other friendly kingdoms. He also fortified the borders and built a series of strongholds in strategic locations. These measures not only protected the kingdom from external threats but also demonstrated the king's commitment to the safety and well-being of his people.

Despite the ongoing challenges, King Nedunchezhiyan remained dedicated to the welfare of his subjects. He introduced various reforms to improve agriculture, ensuring that the fields were fertile and the farmers well-supported. The king also encouraged the development of arts and sciences, believing that a prosperous kingdom was one where knowledge and creativity flourished.

Among the many achievements of King Nedunchezhiyan, his contributions to education and culture stood out. The young king was a patron of the arts, and his court was a vibrant center of literary and artistic activity. Poets, musicians, and scholars thrived under his patronage, creating works that would be celebrated for generations.

One of the most notable poets in King Nedunchezhiyan's court was Nakkeerar, whose verses captured the essence of the king's reign and the beauty of the Tamil land. The king himself was known to appreciate poetry, and he often engaged in discussions with the poets and scholars, encouraging them to explore new themes and ideas.

The king's interest in education extended beyond the royal court. He established schools and learning centers across the kingdom, ensuring that children from all backgrounds had access to education. These institutions became nurseries of knowledge, where young minds were nurtured and prepared to contribute to the kingdom's prosperity.

As the years passed, King Nedunchezhiyan's reputation as a wise and just ruler grew. His people adored him, and neighboring kingdoms respected his authority. The king's strategic mind and courageous spirit had not only defended his kingdom but had also laid the foundations for a golden age of peace and prosperity.

One of the key elements of King Nedunchezhiyan's success was his ability to adapt and learn. He was always open to new ideas and innovations, whether in governance, trade, or culture. This open-mindedness allowed the Pandya kingdom to remain dynamic and progressive, always ready to embrace change and growth.

King Nedunchezhiyan's legacy was also shaped by his deep sense of justice and fairness. He believed that a ruler's true strength lay in the happiness and well-being of his people. This belief guided his actions and decisions, earning him the love and respect of his subjects.

As King Nedunchezhiyan approached the later years of his reign, he began to think about the future of his kingdom. He wanted to ensure that the prosperity and peace he had worked so hard to achieve would continue for generations to come. With this in mind, he focused on preparing the next generation of leaders.

The king established a council of young advisors, carefully chosen for their wisdom, integrity, and dedication to the kingdom. These young leaders were trained in various aspects of governance, from military strategy to economic planning. King Nedunchezhiyan personally mentored them, sharing his knowledge and experiences to prepare them for their future roles.

The young advisors soon proved their worth, bringing fresh perspectives and innovative solutions to the challenges facing the kingdom. Under their guidance, the Pandya kingdom continued to thrive, maintaining its position as a beacon of prosperity and culture in the Tamil land.

As the sun set on King Nedunchezhiyan's illustrious reign, the people of the Pandya kingdom reflected on the remarkable journey they had shared with their beloved king. His strategic mind, courageous heart, and unwavering dedication had transformed the kingdom into a land of peace and prosperity.

The legacy of King Nedunchezhiyan lived on in the stories and songs of the Tamil people. His victories in battle, his wisdom in governance, and his love for his people were celebrated in the verses of the great bards. The king's name became synonymous with valor, justice, and wisdom, inspiring future generations to uphold the values he had embodied.

Even in the years after his reign, the impact of King Nedunchezhiyan's leadership continued to shape the destiny of the Pandya kingdom. The alliances he had forged, the reforms he had introduced, and the cultural renaissance he had nurtured all contributed to the enduring strength and resilience of the kingdom.

The story of King Nedunchezhiyan also found its way into the teachings of the great Sangam scholars. These scholars, who had witnessed the king's reign firsthand, documented his achievements and his contributions to the Tamil literary and cultural heritage. Their writings preserved the memory of King Nedunchezhiyan for future generations, ensuring that his legacy would never be forgotten.

One of the most cherished works from this period is the "Maduraikkanci," which provides a detailed account of King Nedunchezhiyan's reign. This literary masterpiece celebrates the king's strategic brilliance, his victories in battle, and his efforts to unite the various regions of the Tamil country. Through these writings, the spirit of King Nedunchezhiyan continues to inspire and educate.

The lessons learned from King Nedunchezhiyan's life and leadership are timeless. They remind us of the importance of courage, wisdom, and compassion in the face of adversity. They teach us that true leadership is about serving the people and ensuring their well-being. And they inspire us to strive for greatness, no matter the challenges we may face.

As the years turned into centuries, the legend of King Nedunchezhiyan became an integral part of the Tamil cultural identity. His story was passed down from generation to generation, becoming a source of pride and inspiration for the Tamil people. Festivals were held in his honor, and his deeds were reenacted in traditional performances and plays.

In schools and homes, children learned about the great king who had ascended the throne at a young age and had led his kingdom to glory. They heard tales of his bravery in battle, his wisdom in governance, and his love for his people. These stories not only entertained but also instilled important values and lessons in the young minds.

The enduring legacy of King Nedunchezhiyan also influenced the arts. Artists and sculptors created magnificent works depicting scenes from his life, capturing the essence of his valor and leadership. These works of art adorned temples, palaces, and public spaces, serving as constant reminders of the king's enduring influence.

The spirit of King Nedunchezhiyan continued to live on in the hearts of his people. His story was not just a tale of a great king but a testament to the enduring power of courage, wisdom, and justice. It reminded the Tamil people of their rich cultural heritage and the values that had shaped their society.

In times of challenge and uncertainty, the story of King Nedunchezhiyan provided a beacon of hope and inspiration. It encouraged people to stand up for what was right, to face their fears with bravery, and to work towards a better future for themselves and their communities. The legacy of King Nedunchezhiyan was a guiding light, illuminating the path to a brighter tomorrow.

As we reflect on the remarkable life of King Nedunchezhiyan, we are reminded of the timeless lessons he imparted. His story teaches us that true greatness lies not in power or wealth but in the strength of character, the depth of wisdom, and the unwavering commitment to justice and compassion. It is a legacy that continues to inspire, even in the modern world.

The tale of King Nedunchezhiyan, the young king who rose to greatness, is a story of resilience, leadership, and the power of unity. His reign marked a golden era in the history of the Pandya kingdom, a time when peace and prosperity flourished under the guidance of a wise and just ruler.

King Nedunchezhiyan's strategic mind and courageous heart set him apart as a leader. His ability to unite various regions and forge strong alliances ensured the stability and growth of his kingdom. His dedication to the welfare of his people and his patronage of the arts and education created a legacy that transcended generations.

As we celebrate the life and achievements of King Nedunchezhiyan, we are reminded of the importance of preserving our cultural heritage and passing down the stories of our ancestors. These stories not only honor the past but also provide valuable lessons for the future. They inspire us to strive for greatness and to uphold the values of courage, wisdom, and justice in our own lives.

The story of King Nedunchezhiyan is a testament to the enduring power of leadership and the impact one individual can have on the course of history. His life serves as a shining example of what it means to be a true leader, one who leads with integrity, wisdom, and a deep sense of responsibility towards their people.

As the children of today listen to the tales of King Nedunchezhiyan, they are transported to a time of great heroes and epic battles. They learn about the importance of bravery and strategic thinking, and they are inspired to dream big and work towards a brighter future.

The legacy of King Nedunchezhiyan continues to live on, not just in the pages of history books but in the hearts and minds of the Tamil people. His story is a reminder that no matter how young or how seemingly insurmountable the challenges, with courage, wisdom, and a steadfast commitment to justice, anyone can achieve greatness.

Chapter Nine

THE COURAGEOUS KING MARAVARMAN SUNDARA PANDYA

Once upon a time in the vibrant land of South India, a courageous king named Maravarman Sundara Pandya ruled the Pandya dynasty. His kingdom, filled with lush forests, sparkling rivers, and magnificent temples, was a place of prosperity and happiness. Sundara Pandya was not just a king; he was a hero, admired and loved by his people for his bravery, wisdom, and dedication.

The tale of Sundara Pandya began when he ascended to the throne in 1216 CE after the tragic death of his elder brother, Jatavarman Kulasekara Pandya. Kulasekara had been a vassal of the powerful Chola King, Kulothunga Chola III. The Cholas had long dominated the region, casting a shadow over the Pandyas. When Kulasekara defied the Cholas, he faced a crushing defeat, and the ancient Pandyan coronation hall in Madurai was burned down. This act of destruction planted the seeds of revenge in young Sundara Pandya's heart.

Sundara Pandya knew he had to restore the honor of his family and free his kingdom from the Chola's grasp. His journey to greatness was filled with challenges and adventures, making him one of the most legendary kings of his time.

Determined to avenge his brother and reclaim the glory of the Pandyas, Sundara Pandya began his reign with a fierce determination. He gathered his loyal soldiers and wise advisors, preparing for the monumental task ahead. Sundara Pandya was not just a king but a brilliant strategist. He knew that to defeat the mighty Cholas, he needed not only strength but also clever tactics.

His first target was the heart of the Chola kingdom. Sundara Pandya launched a swift and powerful invasion, catching the aging Kulothunga Chola III off guard. The Chola king, now in his twilight years, was unprepared for the fierce onslaught. Sundara Pandya's army, driven by the desire to avenge their fallen comrades and reclaim their land, fought valiantly. The cities of Thanjavur and Uraiyur, once symbols of Chola power, fell to the Pandya forces.

As Sundara Pandya's army marched through the Chola kingdom, they celebrated their victories with great joy. The king himself performed a virabisheka, an anointment of heroes, in the very coronation hall of the Cholas. This act symbolized not just a military triumph but also a spiritual and cultural reclaiming of their heritage.

The celebrations continued as Sundara Pandya and his army marched to Chidambaram, a place of great religious significance. Here, Sundara Pandya performed a Thulabaram, a unique form of worship where he offered tribute equal to his weight. This act of devotion endeared him even more to his people, who saw their king as a brave warrior and a devout leader.

However, the Cholas were not ready to accept defeat easily. Kulothunga Chola III, despite his age, sought help from his son-in-law, Veera Ballala II, the Hoysala monarch. Veera Ballala II, a powerful king in his own right, sent his son, Vira Narasimha II, with a formidable army to assist the Cholas. This alliance posed a new threat to Sundara Pandya.

Unfazed by this challenge, Sundara Pandya showed his diplomatic skills. He agreed to restore the Chola kingdom to Kulothunga, but only after the Cholas acknowledged his suzerainty. This clever move not only secured his position but also established the Pandyas as a dominant power in the region.

With the Cholas acknowledging his supremacy, Sundara Pandya turned his attention to strengthening his kingdom. He focused on building a robust administration, promoting trade, and enhancing the welfare of his people. Under his rule, the Pandya kingdom flourished, becoming a beacon of prosperity and culture in South India.

But peace was not to last. In 1225 CE, a group of Odda soldiers from the faraway land of Odisha invaded the Chola heartland and occupied the sacred city of Srirangam. Sundara Pandya, ever the vigilant protector of his realm, swiftly mobilized his forces. He led his soldiers into battle, driving away the invaders and restoring peace to the region.

His bravery on the battlefield was matched by his compassion off it. Sundara Pandya was known for his fairness and generosity. He often visited villages, listening to the grievances of his subjects and ensuring that justice was served. His people loved him dearly, seeing in him not just a king but a guardian and friend.

As the years went by, Sundara Pandya's fame spread far and wide. He formed alliances with other regional powers to strengthen his position. One of his key allies was the Kadava chieftain Kopperunchinga I. Together, they posed a formidable challenge to both the Cholas and the Hoysalas.

In 1231 CE, the alliance faced a critical test. Rajaraja Chola III, the new Chola king, was captured by Kopperunchinga. This event triggered a series of conflicts that would once again test Sundara

Pandya's leadership. The Hoysala crown prince, Vira Narasimha II, sent an army to intervene and restore Rajaraja Chola III to the throne. Sundara Pandya, ever the strategist, knew he had to tread carefully.

A fierce battle ensued at Mahendramangalam on the banks of the Kaveri River. Sundara Pandya fought bravely, but the Hoysalas proved to be a tough opponent. In the end, he agreed to restore Rajaraja Chola III to his throne, marking a temporary truce between the warring factions. This peace was solidified through dynastic marriages, ensuring a period of stability in the region.

Despite the challenges and battles, Sundara Pandya's reign was marked by significant achievements. Under his leadership, the Pandyas laid the foundations for what would become the Second Pandyan Empire. This period, stretching from 1215 to 1345 AD, saw the Pandyas rise to unparalleled prominence in South India.

The Pandya kingdom, once overshadowed by the Cholas, now stood as a symbol of resilience and strength. Sundara Pandya's victories were inscribed in temples and monuments, telling the tale of his bravery and dedication for generations to come. His meikeerthi, or royal inscriptions, celebrated his conquests and contributions, ensuring his legacy would never be forgotten.

Sundara Pandya was more than a conqueror; he was a builder of a nation. He encouraged the arts, supported scholars, and promoted cultural activities. Under his patronage, Madurai became a center of learning and culture, attracting poets, artists, and thinkers from across the land. The city flourished, its temples and palaces standing as testaments to a golden era of the Pandya dynasty.

Sundara Pandya's love for his kingdom extended beyond its borders. He was known for his diplomatic skills, forging alliances with neighboring kingdoms through marriages and treaties. These alliances not only strengthened his position but also ensured peace and prosperity for his people.

One of his notable achievements was the construction of grand temples and public works. The king believed that by investing in infrastructure and religious sites, he could unite his people and inspire a sense of pride in their heritage. The majestic Meenakshi Temple in Madurai, with its towering gopurams and intricate carvings, stands as a testament to his vision and dedication.

As a ruler, Sundara Pandya was also deeply committed to justice. He established a fair legal system, ensuring that even the poorest of his subjects had access to justice. His court was open to all, and his judgments were known for their fairness and wisdom. The people saw in him a just and benevolent ruler, someone who cared for their well-being and worked tirelessly to improve their lives.

The king's dedication to his kingdom was also evident in his efforts to protect it from external threats. Sundara Pandya maintained a strong and well-equipped army, ready to defend the realm at a moment's notice. His soldiers were loyal and well-trained, inspired by the king's own bravery and leadership on the battlefield.

In one memorable encounter, a coalition of enemy forces threatened to invade the Pandya kingdom. Sundara Pandya, displaying his characteristic courage and strategic acumen, led his army into battle. The clash was fierce, with both sides fighting valiantly. However, under the king's leadership, the Pandya forces emerged victorious, securing the kingdom's borders and ensuring the safety of its people.

Sundara Pandya's legacy extended beyond his military victories and administrative reforms. He was a patron of education and knowledge, establishing schools and libraries to promote learning. He believed that a well-educated populace was key to a strong and prosperous kingdom. His efforts to spread knowledge and wisdom earned him the respect and admiration of scholars and students alike.

As Sundara Pandya grew older, he began to think about the future of his kingdom. He wanted to ensure that the prosperity and peace he had worked so hard to achieve would continue long after his reign. To this end, he focused on grooming his successors and instilling in them the values of courage, wisdom, and dedication.

The king often held councils with his advisors and family, discussing matters of state and the future of the Pandya dynasty. He emphasized the importance of unity and cooperation, knowing that internal strife could weaken the kingdom and make it vulnerable to external threats. His wise counsel and foresight laid the groundwork for a smooth transition of power and continued stability.

In his later years, Sundara Pandya became a beloved figure not just for his accomplishments but also for his humility and kindness. He spent more time among his people, visiting villages and listening to their stories. The king's presence brought joy and comfort to his subjects, who saw him as a fatherly figure and a symbol of hope and strength.

The end of Sundara Pandya's reign marked the beginning of a new era for the Pandya kingdom. His legacy was not just one of military conquests and political achievements, but also of cultural and social advancements. Under his rule, the Pandya dynasty had risen from the shadows of the Cholas to become a dominant force in South India.

Sundara Pandya's successors continued to build on his foundations, expanding the kingdom's influence and fostering a sense of unity and pride among the people. The traditions and values he had instilled in his court and his subjects endured, guiding the kingdom through times of prosperity and challenges alike.

The story of Maravarman Sundara Pandya, the courageous king, is one of resilience, dedication, and visionary leadership. His life and achievements serve as an inspiration to generations, reminding them of the importance of courage, wisdom, and compassion in the face of adversity. The tale of this great king continues to be told and retold, capturing the hearts and minds of those who hear it, ensuring that his legacy lives on forever.

As the years passed, Sundara Pandya's story became a cherished part of the Pandya kingdom's history. Parents would tell their children tales of the brave king who fought valiantly to protect his land and his people. These stories were filled with lessons of bravery, determination, and the importance of standing up for what is right.

In schools, children would learn about Sundara Pandya's victories and his wise rule. They would recite poems and songs that celebrated his life, and reenact scenes from his battles in school plays. Sundara Pandya became a symbol of the virtues that every Pandya citizen aspired to embody.

Even in the distant future, the legacy of Sundara Pandya continued to influence the culture and values of the region. Festivals were held in his honor, where people would come together to celebrate their heritage and the achievements of their ancestors. Temples dedicated to the king and his deities became places of pilgrimage, where devotees would seek blessings and inspiration.

The Pandya kingdom thrived, thanks to the strong foundations laid by Sundara Pandya. His emphasis on education and justice continued to bear fruit, with new generations growing up to be knowledgeable, fair-minded, and dedicated to the welfare of their community.

Trade and commerce flourished under the stable and prosperous conditions that Sundara Pandya had established. Merchants from far and wide visited the Pandya kingdom, bringing with them exotic goods and new ideas. The bustling markets and vibrant cultural exchanges made the kingdom a hub of activity and innovation.

Sundara Pandya's architectural legacy also endured. The grand temples, palaces, and public buildings he commissioned stood the test of time, their beauty and craftsmanship admired by all who saw them. These structures not only served practical purposes but also inspired awe and reverence, reminding everyone of the greatness of their ancestors and the enduring strength of their kingdom.

The arts and literature flourished in the Pandya kingdom, thanks to the patronage and encouragement that Sundara Pandya had provided. Poets, musicians, and artists found a welcoming environment in his court, where their talents were nurtured and celebrated. The king's own love for literature and the arts set a precedent for his successors, who continued to support and promote cultural endeavors.

Under Sundara Pandya's influence, the kingdom became a center of cultural and intellectual activity. Scholars from different regions came to Madurai to study and share their knowledge. The city's libraries were filled with manuscripts on various subjects, ranging from philosophy and science to literature and history.

The king's commitment to preserving and promoting the Tamil language and culture was particularly noteworthy. He recognized the importance of maintaining a strong cultural identity, and his efforts ensured that the rich traditions and heritage of the Pandya kingdom were passed down through the generations.

Sundara Pandya's reign also saw significant advancements in agriculture and infrastructure. The king implemented innovative irrigation systems that improved farming productivity and ensured a steady supply of food for his people. The construction of roads and bridges facilitated trade and communication, connecting different parts of the kingdom and fostering a sense of unity and cohesion.

The king's policies promoted economic growth and social stability. He encouraged the development of industries and crafts, providing artisans and workers with the resources and support they needed to thrive. This economic prosperity translated into a higher standard of living for the people, who enjoyed the benefits of a well-governed and flourishing kingdom.

Throughout his reign, Sundara Pandya remained deeply committed to the welfare of his subjects. He believed that a just and compassionate ruler could create a prosperous and harmonious society. His actions reflected this belief, earning him the love and respect of his people. Sundara Pandya's legacy is a testament to the enduring power of good leadership and the positive impact it can have on a community.

As the sun set on Sundara Pandya's illustrious reign, the Pandya kingdom stood as a beacon of strength, wisdom, and cultural richness in South India. The king's life was a shining example of how determination, courage, and compassion could transform a kingdom and leave a lasting legacy.

Generations that followed looked back at Sundara Pandya's era with admiration and gratitude. His story was told in countless homes, schools, and temples, each retelling keeping the spirit of the courageous king alive. The lessons of his life continued to inspire young and old alike, reminding them of the values that build a strong and just society.

The Pandya kingdom, under the shadow of its heroic king, continued to flourish, its people living in peace and prosperity. Sundara Pandya's name became synonymous with greatness, a symbol of the timeless virtues of bravery, wisdom, and dedication. His story, passed down through the ages, ensured that the memory of the courageous king would never fade, and his legacy would live on in the hearts and minds of his people forever.